LEAVING ANNWN

Returning to Earth on a Mission!

by

Owen Jones

Copyright

Copyright © Owen Jones 2025

ISBN: 978-1-0683538-5-7

Published by Megan Publishing Services
https://meganpublishingservices.com

Disclaimer

This novel is a work of fiction. Names, characters, businesses, places, events, and incidents are either the product of the author's imagination or used in a fictitious manner. Any resemblance to actual persons, living or dead, or actual events is purely coincidental.

The author has made every effort to portray the characters, settings, and events in this book accurately and in a manner consistent with the storyline. However, creative liberties may have been taken for the sake of the narrative.

Readers are reminded that the characters and events depicted in this novel are entirely fictional, and any similarities to real individuals, whether living or deceased, or actual occurrences are unintentional.

The author and publisher disclaim any liability, loss, or risk incurred as a consequence, directly or indirectly, of the use and application of any contents of this novel. Any resemblance to persons, living or dead, events, or locales is entirely coincidental.

Owen Jones

Books in the Annwn – Heaven Series

A Night in Annwn
The Strange Story of Old Willy Jones' NDE

-

Life in Annwn
The Story of Willy Jones' Afterlife

-

Leaving Annwn
Returning to Earth on a Mission

Contact Details

BlueSky: owen-author.bsky.social
Facebook: AngunJones
Instagram: owen_author
LinkedIn: owencerijones
Pinterest: owen_author
TikTok: @owen_author
X: @owen_author
Blog: Megan Publishing Services

Join our newsletter for insider information
on Owen Jones' books and writing
by adding your email to:
https://meganpublishingservices.com

Inspirational Quotes

Believe not in anything simply because you have heard it,
Believe not in anything simply because it was spoken and rumoured by many,
Believe not in anything simply because it was found written in your religious texts,
Believe not in anything merely on the authority of teachers and elders,
Believe not in traditions because they have been handed down for generations,
But after observation and analysis, if anything agrees with reason and is conducive to the good and benefit of one and all, accept it and live up to it.

Gautama Buddha

Great Spirit, whose voice is on the wind, hear me.
Let me grow in strength and knowledge.
Make me ever behold the red and purple sunset.
May my hands respect the things you have given me.
Teach me the secrets hidden under every leaf and stone, as you have taught people for ages past.
Let me use my strength, not to be greater than my brother, but to

fight my greatest enemy – myself.

Let me always come before you with clean hands and an open heart, that as my Earthly span fades like the sunset, my Spirit shall return to you without shame.

(Based on a traditional **Sioux** prayer)

"I do not seek to walk in the footsteps of the Wise People of old; I seek what they sought".
Matsuo Basho

"Have I not commanded you? Be strong and courageous. Do not be afraid; do not be discouraged, for the LORD your God will be with you wherever you go".
Joshua 1:9

"Whatever misfortune befalls you [people], it is because of what your own hands have done- God forgives much-"
Quran 42:30

Myself when young did eagerly frequent
Doctor and Saint, and heard great Argument
About it and about; but oft-times
Came out, by the same Door as in I went.
Omar Khayyam
The Rubaiyat XXIX.

Table of Contents

LEAVING ANNWN i
Copyright ii
Books in the Annwn - Heaven Series iii
Contact Details iv
Inspirational Quotes v
Table of Contents vii
1. An Evening Stroll 1
2. The Akashic Record 13
3. Preliminary Assessment 25
4. Becky Past and Present 37
5. Karma 49
6. Freedom Beckons 61
7. The Patel's 69
8. Entente Cordiale 79
9. The Teenage Years 89
10. Remembrance 101
11. The Star Project 111
12. Unforeseen Developments 119
13. Crisis? What Crisis? 129
14. Two Ends, and Two Beginnings 139
15. The End of an Era? 145
16. Life Goes On 151
Glossary 157

FATE TWISTER..159
About the Author..171
Books by the same author..173
Review Request...177

1. An Evening Stroll

"The place looks so different these days, doesn't it, Sarah?"

"Yes, my dear… life seems dismal and disappointing to so many people. I haven't seen such a general feeling of depression since the time of the Great Plague. It is so sad, Willy".

"Mmm, the last bubonic plague to strike Britain… So many of us worked for so long to help relieve the suffering in those days, but it seemed so much easier back then. There was more, er hope, I suppose than in these days".

"People had more strongly-held religious beliefs in the 14th Century even though between seventy-five and two hundred million people died. Although many of the religious leaders were hypocrites, the people really did believe in God and an Afterlife. It's not the same any more. People find it dispiriting to think that the daily grind is all there is to life".

"Not only has work become less-well paid for most people, but there is a lot of uncertainty with Zero-Hours Contracts, firms going bankrupt and impoverished Social Services. Many people are not only working longer hours, or having two jobs, but they are still worse off than ten years ago. The poor and the needy feel abandoned and ripped-off by the State and the rich people who run it".

"Winter is beginning to set in, yet look at all the people begging and even sleeping on the streets, Sarah!"

"Christmas is on its way, but the place reminds me more of a city of refugees on the edge of a battle zone".

"There has not been such a financial discrepancy between the Have's and the Have-not's in Britain since the Victorian Era, but like I said, people had more religious belief – more hope – in those days. Mankind is in this sad state of affairs despite the massive effort Spirit is making to help people see The Truth".

"Sarah, there are Spirit Guides and Helpers everywhere, but so few of these poor people realise that they are never really alone especially when times are rough. No matter how long I do this work, it still gets to me. How long has it been now? Do you remember? You're better at dates than I am".

"You passed away only a short time ago, and you started helping right away, because you recovered from your life on Earth so quickly".

"Just a few years ago! Sometimes, it seems much longer and yet, at other times, the period has flown past. I know that providing comfort to the afflicted is necessary and worthwhile, but… it can be so depressing too. Yes, I hate to say it, but sometimes, it cheeses me off that so few people actually listen when I talk to them. It makes me want to pack it all in… sometimes, just sometimes".

"Many of us feel like that from time to time, Willy, but you have to keep your eyes on the long term. Even if you only get through to a few Souls, those people will tell others and word gets around that there is Life After Death. Every single one that you remind that reincarnation exists could rekindle the light in dozens of others".

"I know, I know! That's the only thing that keeps me going most of the time".

"Well, it is true that not all of us see a project through to the end… a few Spirit Guides give up on their charges for one reason or another…"

"I, for one, am not surprised! It is demoralising when you are constantly trying to talk with someone, but they never, never, ever seem to be listening!"

"I know, but it's usually not because they are not listening, but because they cannot hear you. Spirit Guides that give up should never have been selected for the job in truth though".

"OK, I can see that, but there are those living on The Surface who do know about their Spirit Guides, but still refuse to listen!"

"Yes, there are those too, but you always have to remember that everyone - 'Dead or Alive', so to speak, has free choice. No-one can force anyone to do or believe anything. Persuasion is the name of the game, and some people are just not very persuasive Nevertheless, there are many other types of work that those people can do, as you well know".

"Like working with animals, you mean?"

"Amongst others, yes. You still enjoy working with abused and neglected animals, don't you?"

"Yes, of course I do, Sarah! You know, I do, but then animals are aware of us – it is more satisfying, as far as that goes".

"Yes, however, you are talking to the converted when you're dealing with animals. It is more challenging to work with humans, and ultimately, more rewarding too, but I agree that the work doesn't suit everyone. You have… are doing well, but perhaps direct contact with people is not really your forte, which is why being a shepherd suited you so well".

"Oh, I'm not giving up! It's just that I understand how disheartening it can be for some. It is not an easy job, Yes, it is rewarding to see someone notice you, but it happens so infrequently these days".

"This is indeed an extremely materialistic period in time, perhaps, the most materialistic ever. There are forces at work encouraging materialism because it suits their Earthly goals. These are very rich, selfish, amoral people, who will go to any lengths to grab more money and more power for themselves to the cost of anyone… However, they are Spirit too, so even with them, there is a chance that they will see The Light.

"I'll tell you something. If you think that working to help the poor and needy is difficult, try making the rich and greedy change their ways. That really is depressing!"

"I can imagine, and I know you try, Sarah. I couldn't do it, I despise the super greedy… and I know that that's wrong too, but I can't help it".

"No, not yet, my darling, but I know that you can see that if even one as advanced as yourself can't stomach the super selfish, then it is not surprising that many of those who need our help can't see us too… and there are people working on you too to help you get over your prejudice against the super greedy".

"I know. People like you, for a start… and our Becky. She is so much like you".

"We have worked together for a very long time… many centuries before we decided that she should be born our daughter on The Surface, and that we should become an Earthly team".

"I remember you telling me that before, and I believe you, of course, but I never have understood how that useless husband of hers, er, John, wasn't it, fitted into the picture".

"Oh, John is one of Becky's most promising students, but he was worried about being reborn on The Surface again, so Becky offered to allow him to join up with her on Earth to help him settle in. He did his best, love".

"I suppose so. Not my type either though, I'm afraid".

"He vibrates at a different – OK, lower – level to you. That's why, and you know that, so you ought to try harder. And while we're on the subject, that is why you can't stomach the super greedy too – they just vibrate far too low beneath you. There is no resonance… you and they are out of harmony in the most basic of ways. The discord is so great that you can't bear their company. They are mostly too base to understand you on that level, but they hate the things you say, which represent everything that makes them feel uneasy. People like you make them feel uncomfortable, so they retaliate against you – even try to hurt you.

"You need to learn to rise above that, because they can only hurt your physical body. Still, all in good time, eh? Walking through the centre of Cardiff after nightfall really is like being in a war zone, isn't it?" said Sarah as they walked up the shopping precinct called Queen Street towards Cardiff Castle, suspended a foot off the ground.

"This is the most prosperous area of the city with its symbols of power – the government buildings and the castle – and yet look around us… it seems 'cold' too – impersonal, unhelpful, and unyielding… It will get much colder in temperature too over the coming months, before it becomes warmer again. I suppose many of the poor sods we see here will be back with us in Annwn by then though".

"They aren't 'poor sods', Willy, as well you know! They chose to be reborn to follow a course that interested them when they were in Annwn. It just so happens that these Dark Times are conducive to learning harsh lessons and many people are taking advantage of it".

"Yes, I know. They actually came to The Surface to learn how to deal with sleeping on the streets…"

"Well, among many other things, yes, but that is one of the hardest lessons to learn. Not sleeping on the streets, I mean, but remembering that we chose our course on Earth ourselves before we came back up here".

"It is hard to tell people that they are being blown up or sleeping rough because they chose to though, isn't it?"

"Yes, and it is hard to remember that the super rich and greedy have chosen to play those rôles in their university course on The Surface too… they are only acting out a part in a play".

"OK, point taken. I even know it and have done for as long as I can remember, but I cannot keep the idea in the front of my mind".

"It is very difficult, my dear, but then being 'dead' doesn't make you an angel, does? Deciding to study the Laws is one thing, but it is another to actually remember them, and *then* it takes lifetimes to learn how to live by them".

"I know, but we will all get there in the end".

"You could express it that way, although I prefer to think of it as 'as one day', because there is no end that I know of… eternity is infinite, surely?"

"I can't argue with that, Sarah. One thing I do know, is that I am so glad that I have you on my side. I am a very lucky man. You know, I never get tired of talking to you – even when you are trying to teach me. That has to be a sign of a top educator, but I have always known that you are far more advanced than I. I even knew it when we were married in our little cottage on the Brecon Beacons and I kept you so busy that you were virtually housebound. I was cruel to you, but you never complained, you just got on with your work and held our family together".

"You couldn't hear what I used to say about you when you were in the pub!", she laughed.

"Perhaps, but I'm not sure that I believe you on that score… You were always my guiding light, and I knew it even then, although I had forgotten that I had known you before in Annwn. Did you remember Annwn before we married on The Surface?"

"No, I can't say that I did. I didn't really know about Annwn then either. I called it Heaven like everyone else did, but I did feel a strong attraction to the mountains I could see out of our back-kitchen window… beyond our back-garden. I would talk to them when I was doing the washing-up or the laundry. I loved being in our garden most of all though. It made me feel free. I knew that you and Kiddy were on our little mountain tending the sheep not far away, and I wanted to be out there too".

"I'm sorry for being such a pig, my darling".

"You have said that many times since, Willy, and I know you mean it. I knew it wasn't the real you doing it then too… You were only doing what you needed to do to get through the day. You were a good husband during hard times, and you never went astray or left us wanting".

"They were hard times, but I can't help thinking that these are even harder than then. Despite the religious aspect, we grew up after the Great Depression and the Second World War, they were times of great hope for the future. That hope is lacking now, sadly lacking, you might say.

"Money is scarce…"

"It always has been for people like us!"

"Yes, but our generation could buy our own homes, kids these days can't. We could travel… well, not you and me, because of the sheep, but it was easy because of the European Union, but kids now have seen that dragged away from them too. Not only that, but we could retire at sixty-five and the youth of today will have to work until they are seventy or even seventy-five. We had the chance of a free university education too, or our Becky did, and now even that's gone! Expensive further education, low wages, difficult travel and rented accommodation – that's what our kids lave to look forward to… AND and extra ten years of work.

"I'm not surprised they're angry, me!"

"No, I know you're not. You have a good heart… but a poor memory. Those kids, as you keep calling them, are taking advantage of the current times to learn the lessons that it has to offer, and they include hardship. Which is something the poor, or the relatively poor, have always had to bear, even in this rich country. It is much worse in most other countries, don't forget".

"I know, I know, but I can't help feeling that it's not right…"

"Well, it is right, otherwise those courses would not be available at this beautiful university that we call Earth".

"I know, I do know, really. You are right, I know that you are, but I still cannot live that lesson".

"You will, Willy, one day, you will – everyone will - but knowing it and living it are totally different kettles of fish. Let me give you a kiss, you great big softie. Have you had enough? Do you want to go home, my dear?"

"I have had enough, and I do want to go home, my dear. You can read my Aura, but you would know anyway… you know me better than I know myself, but I want to walk and talk a little longer. I want to learn the lessons you try to teach me… I want to be a successful student… to make you proud of me".

"Please don't talk like that, my love. I am proud of you. I always have been, and I cannot imagine that there will ever come a day when I will not be, but it is good for you to progress. You know what is right, but, as you yourself say, you cannot accept what you know, or, in your own words, you cannot yet live that life. Your beloved kids would probably say that you can talk the talk, but not yet walk the walk", she said smiling into his face. Willy put his arms around his wife and kissed her.

"You always know just what to say", he said squeezing her again and releasing her.

"We should be lending a hand, I suppose", said Willy taking Sarah's hand and walking on.

"Only if we want to", she replied. "We are allowed to have time to ourselves too. There is no-one to say what anyone has to do or should be doing. No-one will ever criticise us even if we never help anyone ever again. You know that too".

"Yes, but there are those who would be very surprised if you packed it all in and went to live on a deserted paradise planet, aren't there?"

"Yes, I suppose there are!" she laughed, "but that sort of life wouldn't suit you either, would it? Not in the long run. You and I are very much alike. We want to help… to make a difference… and what we, and the countless of millions of other Spirit Guides, do, does make a difference. You know it does. You could no more sit on a paradise island for the rest of Eternity than I could".

"No, I guess you're right again, but I am a bit world-weary tonight, and don't have the strength to help at the moment, so can we just walk and watch?"

"Of course! However, that's helping too, or it could be. What if one of these late-night shoppers saw us kissing just now? He or she would tell his or her family and friends and that would start people talking about ghosts and life after death, which is what we want – to spark thought".

"We could become a legend – 'The Kissing Ghost Couple of Queen Street'!"

"Oh, yes! But then we would have to come back and do it again on a regular basis – what day is it today? Every Friday night, or every third week in November", she giggled.

"I'd be happy to come back here every night, if it meant a kiss from you".

"What, in the line of duty, you mean?"

"No, in the line of preference… You always were better at words than me".

"I was only joking. Ooh, you are getting maudlin, aren't you? Is all this misery getting to you again?"

"I suppose it is. Sorry, my dear. I should have known you were only joking… and if I didn't know, I should have looked at your Aura".

"You are run down, and you are taking all this to heart", she said squeezing his hand with her right hand and indicating the rough sleepers with her left.

"Yes, you're right, as always, my love, but I really don't want to go home just yet. Let's walk past St. John The Baptist Church and into St. Mary Street. I love that little church – it's Fifteenth Century, I think. It's like an island of Goodness in the surrounding shopping centre of Babylon".

"I know what you mean. I like it too". There was a trestle table outside the small isolated church, where two women and a man were handing out mugs of hot soup ladled from a huge tureen to anyone who asked for some. There was a pile of bread rolls to dip in it too, but no spoons as they had all been stolen on previous evenings. Diners were using their own mugs, which meant that most of the thick pea and ham soup went to those for whom it was intended and not to hungry shoppers. It also satisfied the current anti Covid-19 measures of not sharing cutlery or utensils, which could be used as a reason for not serving just anyone who felt peckish.

"That is a heart-warming sight, isn't it, Sarah? I'm glad that I saw that tonight before going home".

"Look!" said Sarah, pointing to one of the women with her chin and smiling. "That lady there can see us, but she can hardly believe her eyes. Let's give her a big wave and cheery smile". Willy looked over and did as he was bid. The young woman's mouth dropped open as she tried to signal to her colleagues what she could see. Willy and Sarah waited a minute to see whether the others would be able to see them as well, but moved on when it became obvious that they could not.

"Yes, that has made my day!" said Willy.

"Many people are trying to help, Willy, not only Spirit, although many Surface Dwellers are inspired by Spirit, even if they are well-intentioned anyway. Like those people back there. I looked for a banner to advertise their organisation, but didn't see one. They probably weren't looking for recognition… they just wanted to help".

"Oh, I'm sure that there are people who just want to help. Definitely… In fact, we knew some in the village, didn't we? Er, um… I forget their names now, but there definitely were some".

"Yes, sure there were. There are nice people everywhere. Most of them just need a little nudge in the right direction so that they know that they are not alone. Does that sound familiar? We provide the nudge from our side to those who can see us, and they provide the same sort of nudge to people on their side. We are all working to alleviate suffering; the main difference being that they try to improve lives one day, or even one meal at a time, and we try to change whole lives, or outlooks. We try to teach that there is nothing to fear but fear itself, and that no-one can really harm you because of Life After Death and Re-incarnation".

"I imagine that sometimes a warm meal on a cold night is of more help".

"In the sort term, probably so, but it's like a glutton going on a diet. They soon put the weight back on when they stop dieting. However, if you teach them to love exercise, or how much they are damaging the planet, you may change their way of life for ever so that they can give up dieting. It's the same with compulsive shoppers… and drinkers… most addicts, in fact. They all go for the quick fix to their obsession rather than finding out why they are unhappy and fixing the reason for that instead.

"People treat symptoms instead of curing the illness, and so the problem keeps recurring, requiring another dose of what the patient is addicted to, and then another… ad infinitum, until they meet and listen to, someone like us". Sarah smiled. She was not being sanctimonious or self-righteous, she was simply stating The Truth.

"Do you remember the sadhu Prahlad Jani - the Indian ascetic who claimed to have lived without food and water for several decades, because food was only an addition? Prahlad Jani made headlines by stating that he didn't eat or drink, and to demonstrate his claim, he underwent observation, including being allegedly buried alive for a lengthy period of time. However, that is way beyond the ability of almost everyone who returns to Earth".

"Yes, my darling, well, we can all only do our best, and at the moment I feel dead beat. I think I am ready to go home now and call it a day. Unless you want to carry on…"

"No, no, I can go back too. Tomorrow is another day, and we are not so close to our goal that finishing up for the day will make any difference. Besides, there are many more people still continuing the Good Fight. No, let's just go back home. Ready? One, two, three!"

They were instantaneously standing in their small apartment above the cottage where they had spent all their married life on the small mountain that they called their own. The ground floor of the cottage was a Spiritualist Sanctuary and a village Community Centre now, but they had left the attic so that the donors of the building could use it as a refuge. Willy and Sarah had been using it for this purpose for three decades and Becky sometimes stayed there too. They preferred it to the hustle and bustle of the city of Annwn, or even the quiet of the surrounding countryside. It was their own little cottage, and they were its resident ghosts, whom most of the people who used the building regularly had seen several times.

"It has been a good day", said Sarah, "so you have reason to be worn out. Let's go and lie down to recharge our batteries".

"I'm ready for that", replied Willy as they disappeared into their bedroom and appeared on the bed. The room had all their old furniture, or at least all the items that meant anything to them, although whether they had been there or not would not have mattered to them, as they could easily conjure up anything that they needed or wanted. It had been their daughter Becky's idea to put their stuff in their flat, and they hadn't had the heart to say 'No'. Kiddy, their old sheep dog bounded up onto the bed at their feet.

"There's a good girl, Kiddy", murmured Willy sleepily. "Good night, girl. Good night to you too, Sarah. Let's see what tomorrow brings".

They didn't need to sleep in the way that Surface Dwellers had to – they didn't have bodies that needed rest, but they did need time out. They felt the need to plug into the Universe from time to time, but not necessarily every day. They would usually go their separate ways when they 'rested', but not always, and they didn't always go anywhere.

Rest to them was more like a meditation; a time to gather their thoughts; a time to strengthen their own individual inner peace.

2. The Akashic Record

While Willy was recharging his ability to withstand the stress of witnessing so much misery, he wanted to direct his meditation to the last period of national suffering that he knew anything about – The Bubonic or Great Plague. What bothered him was that he didn't know enough about it, so he decided to consult the Akashic Record, which he had done once before in this cycle, immediately after he had passed over.

The Akashic Record is a memory of everything that has ever happened in the Universe, and he, like most who had recently passed on, had consulted it to review his latest existence on The Surface.

He now wanted to check what part, if any, St John The Baptist's Church in Church Street, Cardiff had played during the Bubonic Plague of 1665-1666. Rightly or wrongly, he thought that there probably hadn't been so many people sleeping on the streets of Cardiff for nearly 400 years.

He had previously checked the Akashic Record in one of the viewing rooms in the University of Annwn, but he had learned, or relearned, a lot since then. He was again able to find out anything in history from any location whatsoever, although he still found it most convenient to imagine himself sitting in a theatre.

He started by ridding his mind of distracting thoughts, since he no-longer had a physical body that needed to be relaxed. It was a technique that he had learned many years before while still living on The Surface, but it still worked just as well in Annwn. He saw himself as an impresario in the cavity where his brain had used to be, and treated every thought as an annoying, but obedient creature. He lined all the thoughts up in the middle of his mind and opened up a fissure in the ground before them.

"We're going to play a game!" he announced to the creatures and commanded them to jump over the crack. The weakest thoughts disappeared into the chasm, and he continued to widen the gap and tell the thought-creatures to jump over it until he was standing alone in his empty head.

He next imagined a row of empty seats, just like in a theatre and sat in one of them before creating a stage and a large screen centre-stage. The only thoughts in his head were openness and reception. There were no distractions. It had taken him decades to be able to perform this feat so quickly.

"I want to consult the Akashic Record about the rôle of St. John The Baptist's Church in Cardiff during the Great Plague of 1665 to 1666", he thought-commanded of no-one in particular. Almost instantaneously, an image formed on the screen. Although the church stood in open ground, it was immediately recognisable. There were none of the modern shops and public houses, although there were stalls, from which people sold food and beer. Most of the vendors appeared to be in fancy dress resembling giant birds… ducks and geese even.

Apart from these stalls, there were other fancy dress characters delivering food and drink to people of all ages and both sexes, who appeared to be lounging around on the ground outside the church. Most were unaccompanied, and most were writhing and groaning. On closer inspection, it became obvious that those lying around were sick, some had black or greying skin – the result of gangrene, and others were already dead. It was a warm day, and clouds of flies were gathering over some of the corpses. The Akashic Record did not provide sound or smell, but those who were not dressed as birds wore neckerchiefs over their noses, so Willy assumed that the smell was bad.

Occasionally, priests and nuns would come out of the church to administer some small comfort to the sick, and the Last Rites to the dying. Suddenly a large bird-creature walked towards his stand-point, and removed his headdress. He tapped it against his leg as he hurried on and limp flowers and herbs fell from the beak or nose cone. The man stopped at a stall and purchased a handful of fresh plants that he stuffed into his mask before returning to his own stall. Willy looked at the stall and could just make out a rudimentary advertisement: 'Medicinal, pungent herbs and flowers – guaranteed to keep the Black Death, and the smell of it at bay! Only a farthing a bunch!'.

Willy returned his attention to the church yard and the streets beyond. A cart pushed by two children was being used to collect the dead. As soon as a body was taken away, somebody hurried to help another plague victim into the vacant spot closer to the church for a price.

Money was being made from the Bubonic Plague – the worst plague to hit Britain during the last four hundred years killing about seventy-five thousand people.

This was not relaxing, so Willy turned the screen off and just imagined nothingness. It was a very welcome relief. The time of the Great Plague had been much worse, but the sight of dozens of bodies lying in the streets was similar to what they had witnessed earlier that evening.

When Willy 'woke up' several hours later, he was alone, so he just remained on the bed and considered his 'dream' about Mediaeval Cardiff during The Plague. He had not witnessed as much as he had hoped to – he still wanted to know more – but it had distressed him, so he would have to return at another time. Suddenly, Kiddy was on the bed licking him and when he looked up, Sarah was smiling at him

"We thought we'd let you have a lie in, so we went down to the garden until we felt you come around. Do you feel better today – more relaxed, I mean?"

"Yes, thank you. I checked the Akashic Record last night for what Cardiff was like during the Great Plague..."

"That couldn't have been very relaxing".

"No, it wasn't, but I didn't stay long. It was quite horrific, and Cardiff was only a small town in those days. I dread to think what places like London must have been like".

"Well, in those days, there weren't any places like London in Britain.

It was a one-off, but it must have been pretty bad, and it might have gotten even worse if it hadn't been for The Great Fire of London in 1666 killing off lots of the rats and their fleas that were spreading The Plague".

"But The Great Fire would not have helped any other town or city, would it. I wonder what brought The Plague to an end outside London".

"I don't know, Willy, and I don't know how you would find out… It would certainly take a great deal of research, not that that is an obstacle, if you have the patience". Kiddy looked up, barked and leaped through the wall. "I see that we have visitors… some of the villagers coming to open up The Sanctuary, no doubt. Do you want to go downstairs and see what's going on, or stay here a while longer?"

"I'll join you in a moment, my dear".

"OK, à bientôt, my dear", and Sarah vanished too.

Willy moved to the window, imagined a seat, sat down and looked out over his old front garden and the road. Beyond that, the mountain rose up before him and blocked his view, although he knew what lay there. He knew every square inch of their mountain.

He watched a few people he recognised get out of the car. One of them spotted him before he had time to duck behind the curtain and she waved at him. Reluctantly, he waved back, and he saw his wife and dog appear a little way from the new arrivals. Sarah followed the direction of the wave, and knew instantly that her husband regretted having been seen, but she did not withhold the smile that burst onto her face. Willy saw it to, as she waved at him as well. He held up his hand in recognition and retired to the bed again. Luckily, the upstairs apartment had been put off-limits to everyone but Becky decades ago, so he knew that he would not be disturbed.

∞

"I would like to do more to help the youth of this country", said Willy to Sarah when they met up in the garden several hours later. "The only problem is that I have no idea how best to go about it. What do you think, my dear?"

"At any given moment, Spirit as a whole is doing all that it can, but that sum total can be increased if any one person decides to do more", she replied logically. "If you want to do more, I will help you and work with you to accomplish that. I'm afraid that's all I can say to you at the moment… We need to talk… with each other, and perhaps Becky, and perhaps others in the University. Becky has been involved with helping the homeless since shortly after you arrived here. What do you say?"

"Yes, we can do that, starting with just the two of us as soon as you have time".

"I always have time for you… or I will make it. Shall we go back into Cardiff and maybe a few other out-lying towns soon to assess the situation?"

"OK, I knew you would know what to do".

∞

"So, Becky, that's the long and the short of it. Your mother, I mean, Sarah, and I have been taking a closer interest in the problems of the day in the UK recently and we think that we would like to do more to help. I understand that you are already involved, or not? What do you think?"

"Yes, it is my pet project. Britain has been in local wars since the Second World War, but there hasn't been the massive disruption in the UK that war causes for many decades… However, that doesn't mean that the population is not undergoing a kind of psychological turmoil. The people's trust in their leaders took a massive hit with the Expenses Scandal among politicians, and one could say that a lot of the current Angst stems from there. Then there was the Banking Crisis, Austerity, the crisis of Child Abuse within the Church, Brexit, and now Covid-19.

"You could easily say that the Pillars of Family Life, Society and the Financial World have been seen to crumble, and all in such a short period of time… and there is more to come. Nepotism in public companies like the BBC, corruption, the National Health Service Crisis, the systematic impoverishment of the Working Classes, legalised tax evasion, the housing shortage, and much, much more. It will all come to light over time, and none of that news will serve to calm the people… quite the opposite. I am afraid that things will probably get much worse before they start to get better. Brexit doesn't help either, since it gives the Ruling Classes more opportunity to exploit the population without the regulatory control of the European Union. In short, at the moment, the hands of the British Ruling Classes are still somewhat tied, but Brexit will allow them to free themselves, I'm afraid.

"I think that the people of Britain will soon need our help more than at any time since World War II. What do you propose to do about it?"

"We are unsure, darling. We wanted to run it past you before we did anything", said Sarah.

"OK, well, let me see… the first thing that comes to mind, is that the three of us could concentrate our efforts more in that direction, but that would of necessity mean withdrawing services from elsewhere. The second line would be to get out there and try to drum up support around the sensitives in the Cardiff area, or whichever area you intend concentrating on; and the third thing, off the top of my head, would be to formulate a long term plan and get yourselves reborn into positions where you can help from the inside so to speak…"

"You mean re-incarnate?"

"Yes, I know that it has not been long since you returned to Annwn, so you might not be up to full strength yet, but you might not have to go back to The Surface for long, if you had a good enough plan…"

"Start a movement and die young, you mean?" asked Willy.

"Yes, it has worked on other occasions… many occasions… Think of Jesus, for example".

"I don't think I could aim as high as Jesus!" said Willy.

"OK, it was only an example… Martin Luther King, or one of the millions of others over the millennia".

"It is a way, Willy. You, or we, might not even have to wait that long.

There have been thousands of cases where the seemingly needless death of a child, or even a baby, has sparked social change. It all has to do with planning", advised Sarah.

"Yes, I suppose it does, but could we really pull it off?"

"We will never know if we don't try", said Sarah.

"Well. I'm up for it!" announced Willy. "I mean, if that suits everyone else".

The ladies looked at each other, smiled and nodded in unison. "We're in!" they said.

∞

They decided that Sarah and Willy would carry out most of the initial surveillance to determine the exact needs of the local community, and that Becky would try to convince the circle she worked with in her parents' old cottage to get out on the streets of Cardiff to meet the homeless and disgruntled youth in general, in order to ascertain what the problems facing them were.

Despite the distance from the village to the capital, members of the community centre and the Development Circle decided to go to Cardiff en masse at least once a week in order to hand out leaflets stating the exact locations of free kitchens and sleeping places, and to talk to kids hanging around on the streets in the city centre.

The leaflets for the homeless were an immediate success; so much so that they led to the free sleeping places soon filling up, although the soup kitchens run by the Salvation Army and several other organisations welcomed the increase in numbers too. Becky's band of helpers also tried to organise the donation of food suitable for sandwiches to the homeless and other comestibles that needed cooking to the so-called soup kitchens, although some actually provided proper meals.

Trying to form bonds with groups of bored, suspicious teenagers proved to be rather less successful, and they learned little more than they already knew, which was that the kids had no money, nowhere to go, and nothing to occupy their time, since most of the youth centres had been closed because of the lack of centralised spending due to austerity measures. Covid-19 was not helping either, as it seemed to give legitimacy to the closures.

It was uncertain whether the cuts caused by the austerity measures would not have been imposed by other political parties as well, but it was true that the Conservative Party had implemented them, and many said with too much relish. It was a matter of personal opinion, since political party allegiances frequently ran along family, and not logical lines.

Meanwhile, Sarah and Willy spent a great deal of time studying the Akashic Records to learn how other nations were handling their versions of the same and similar crises. The huge influx into mainland Europe of refugees from Afghanistan, Syria and northern Africa in general provided some pointers, but neither Sarah nor Willy liked the idea of barbed-wire camps for the homeless, although the threat of it coming to that had obviously been considered by the Conservative government of the day.

The Press blamed the influx of foreigners for the housing shortage, and many people took this as a given fact, especially when there were thousands of refugees on French shores trying to smuggle themselves into Britain every day. Many died trying, either in flimsy rubber boats on the English Channel or in refrigerated lorries arriving in England. Recently thirty-nine young Vietnamese hopefuls had frozen or suffocated to death in one container. People could not understand why anyone would risk their lives to get to the UK when wages, housing and social security benefits were far better where they were in France, but the newspapers kept saying that the UK was one of the best countries in Europe. It was lies, but Brits wanted to believe it, and non-Europeans knew no better.

So, they kept coming, fuelling the anti-foreigner debates. The close, but poor working-class families of the North-east and South Wales proved to be fertile grounds for the nationalistic, and some would say, xenophobic, Reform Party and its forerunner, the United Kingdom Independence Party or UKIP.

However, the debates weren't helping because foreigners were not the cause of the problem – they were a distraction to paper over bad government and a greedy Ruling Class.

This made planning an effective strategy to help the nation very difficult indeed.

∞

The former Jones family of Bryn Teg mountain met often to compare notes and build up a dossier on how best to help the people of the UK. However, life went on for the family members, and they all had things to do - commitments and obligations. Willy was still comforting neglected animals, especially pets, that were being mistreated either wilfully or through ignorance; Sarah had her classes, where she both taught and studied; and Becky was involved with the homeless of Cardiff, and several Spiritualist Development Circles, The Circles were usually, but not always, attached to Spiritualist Churches and aimed to give training and confidence to psychics of all strengths and types.

Sarah and Willy also had meetings with specialists at placing those who wanted to be reborn with people already on The Surface, who were hoping to have a child. Many Spirits made their own long-term arrangements before they were reborn – friends or people who had been family before often decided to continue their associations on a rolling basis, which meant that many Souls were reborn into the same regions for hundreds or even thousands of years. However, there were also those people who changed their minds and wanted children after they had been reborn. Willy and Sarah were considering looking for such a couple in the Cardiff area.

"So, what is your intention, Willy?" asked Steven, a member of the support staff in Annwn.

"We are not quite sure yet, Steven, but the situation in the UK is currently so bad that we would like to do all we can to help".

"Yes, I see… but you haven't made prior arrangements to be reborn with a family currently on The Surface?"

"No, it was a recent idea. We were walking through Cardiff the other day and were appalled at the number of homeless sleeping on the streets and the overwhelming sense of hopelessness. We just thought that we would like to help, didn't we, dear?"

"Yes… It is something that we… and a friend of ours, would like to do together".

"And the three of you would like to be born together into the same family at the same time?"

"I don't know about that, we haven't given it a lot of thought, have we Willy? Our friend, Becky, was our daughter in our last incarnations".

"I see. Well, it is possible for you to be triplets, of course, because of the modern use of fertility drugs. Triplets are quite common these days… even quadruplets or quintuplets… Anyway, if you wanted to use the same arrangement that you had last time, you would obviously have to be born first, wait about twenty Earth years for maturity and then wait another, well, say fifteen years in order to be able to act as an effective team, and by then, the crisis might be over".

"Yes. I can see that…" muttered Willy. "Thirty-five years… one would hope that the crisis would be over long before then for sure. What do you think, Sarah?"

"I think that if we wait thirty-five years we will overshoot the problems that we want to help with. However, there will always be something to do. I think that we ought to go back and have another chat with Becky. She may have another perspective".

"Yes, you're right. All right, Steven, thanks for all your help and time. We'll get back to you soon".

"Yes, thanks for everything, Steven".

"Any time, I am here to help".

∞

"So, that's the position, Becky".

"Well, we can't be born into the past, so the clock is ticking… so to speak".

"No, we can't. More's the pity! It's one of the immutable Laws", replied Sarah.

"So, if we, or some of us, want to be re-born, Steven and his team are confident that they can find us suitable parents?"

"Yes".

"But we can also use the Akashic Record to find our own parents… or we could be born as neighbours or cousins. That would involve even more 'parents' sympathetic to our goals. I mean, if we are all born into one family, we would have a maximum of two parents to help us, but we could have six… or even more, what with step-parents…"

"Yes, or we could just choose a large family", offered Willy. "There are lots of options, and I'm sure that after we have thought about it a bit more, we can make better use of Steven's time and understand his advice more easily".

"I agree", interjected Becky, "but how long do we think that this current crisis will last? In other words, how long do we have before it is not worth going there for that?"

"Who knows? But Willy and I have been looking into the housing crisis and it will take at least twenty years to sort that out. As for the crisis of confidence, well, how long is a piece of string, but I personally think that politicians and the rich will never be trusted as much again as they they were in the decades after the Second World War. The working classes have never trusted the rich and their political spokespeople, but they did seem to from the War until the expenses scandal and then the Banking Crisis. It was an eye-opener for a new generation… a couple of generations, probably.

"So, I think that we are on the threshold of exciting times, when average people take control of their own futures… or will want to. Of course, the ruling classes might not like this and may try to distract people by starting more wars or carrying out other acts that minds like ours can't imagine. In fact, I will be surprised if they just roll over and go to the Bahamas".

"Social unrest?" asked Willy.

"Could be. Elections are coming soon, and so will a total Brexit… but who knows whether they will alleviate or exacerbate the situation?"

"And if things turn out bad, it could mean troops on the streets and civil unrest like in the USA…" said Becky in a low voice, "and if that happens, it will not be over quickly, and we will wish that we had taken action while we had the chance".

"Well, that's it then!" exclaimed Willy. "We have to try to help! I'm up for reincarnation".

"I agree that we have to try to help, but I'm not sure yet what is best for us to do. Should we all be reborn? Or how many? Perhaps, it would be better to keep one of us here as a co-ordinator", suggested Sarah.

They stepped out onto the hill outside the cottage and drifted up to its peak. Not a word more was spoken, but they all knew that they were going to start a mission soon that they hoped would help their fellow country folk and perhaps have an even wider affect.

The wind was blowing cold, but the only chill they felt was worry for the future of the population.

3. Preliminary Assessment

"I suggest that we take a closer look at how people really live in South Wales these days", suggested Becky. "We could look at Cardiff, of course, and, say, Newport to the east of it, Barry to the west, and our beloved Brecon to the north. It will be interesting to compare these completely different towns or cities. You would expect Cardiff to be administrative, Newport to be more industrial, Brecon to be rural and Barry to be more of a holiday resort. Any objections?" Willy and Sarah shook their heads.

"It always amazes me how methodical Becky can be", said Sarah to Willy in a quiet. but very proud voice, as if they were at a school event and she were still her mother.

"Personally, I think that the old-fashioned differences between those municipalities will have become blurred because of the run-down local economies and the International nature of the Internet. Globalism, as they call it… one size fits all. One of the problem with that is that the Internet is dominated by the Americans, and American culture, and the American way of doing business does not suit every society, and this angers many people… indeed, Peoples.

"Some of these people or Peoples rail against having their culture, their individualism eroded or even destroyed, and this causes feelings of anxiety and hopelessness… Especially in the older generations, because they can remember when places were different, but not so much in the young, who know nothing else. Some would say know no better, but that is subjective.

"One thing is for certain, the Internet has the effect of downward pressure on wages. A largish proportion of the uneducated young used to work in shops or supermarkets, but nowadays, many traditional shops are going bankrupt because of Internet shopping and the Coronavirus pandemic. The middle classes are hit by Internet banking and desktop publishing et cetera, et cetera. The list goes on and on. People read online newspapers, so newsagents fail; people bet online, so bookmakers fail; people book holidays online, so travel agencies fail, while most of the online counterparts are almost fully automated creating few real jobs, and even the ones they do create could be in a different country, so not even the government benefits from their taxation.

"As government revenue is slashed, so must government services, so schools, hospitals, infrastructure and social services must be reduced. All of this adds to the depressing effect on the population, who can't see what they have done to deserve a less generous society when only a few decades before, the media was still proclaiming the dawn of a prosperous Golden Age wherein the working week would be reduced without loss of wages because of increased automation.

"Well, the automation has arrived, but it has brought poverty, not riches, so people feel cheated, lied to, and betrayed.

"In my view, this is the main reason for the widespread feeling of hopelessness in society".

"It sounds right, Becky, well done", said Willy, beaming. "Your mother, I mean Sarah, and I missed the dawn of the Internet Era, and don't need computers or the Internet in Annwn, so have never bothered with it, but your summation of the predicament society finds itself in seems to fit the bill".

"I agree", said Sarah, "but there is more. Successive governments failed to predict the need to import labour to pay the pensions of an older nation, or, if they did, it didn't suit their political aspirations to explain it to the people.; So, when immigrants were allowed in to pay taxes to cover the shortfall, there were no houses for them. At best, this was short-sighted of the government, at worst it was selfish because the government looked after landlords who benefit from a shortage of housing, since it keeps the rents higher. Then there is the Spiritual issue too – materialism has got a firm grip on people in the West… and I don't just mean of Wales!" The three smiled at the old stereotypical joke of the mean farmers of West Wales.

"One thing is certain", said Becky, "we are not going to be able to turn back time and destroy the Internet to return us to a state of higher and more well-paid employment".

"No, I don't think either of us would suggest that", said Sarah looking concerned. "No, not at all… The Internet obviously has a potential for good. Look at all the labour – often menial, boring work – that it is taking care of and practically automatically. No, I don't think that the Internet is to blame for anything, on the contrary, it is to be congratulated, or the forces that created it should be.

"As I see it, the government is to blame again. It failed to realise the potential of the Internet and harness it. People were allowed to make vast fortunes, often cornering markets and changing societies… some for the better, I am sure, but as Becky just pointed out, others for the worse. I have seen that people in extremely poor countries can now use the Internet to make cheap telephone calls and thereby do business without middlemen for the first time, but it has had a more dubious effect on more wealthy societies.

"Under certain circumstances, it could be seen to be a good thing that Westerners earn less and the World's poor earn more, but that is not all that is happening. The West is being impoverished and a few dozen large Internet firms, often still in the hands of their male founders, are making billions every week at the expense of our Western conurbations, while paying a disproportionately small amount of tax, because their businesses are run from tax havens.

"Again, as I see it, if we are going to have a global economy run mostly over the Internet or the World Wide Web, then the taxation system should be global too – for Internet companies, anyway. Now, don't ask me how that could be done, but we do have clever people here who could inspire those in power on The Surface, so long as the will of the government is on board. To me, it seems that it isn't, or hasn't been up to this point in time. Were politicians caught napping, or were they paid to look the other way? Who knows? And whoever does know is not saying, at least not to me".

"This would split society", chipped in Willy, "creating an 'us' and a 'them', but the 'them' are no longer the rich and the powerful, 'they' are now the people in the suburbs with the decent jobs - teachers, factory workers, tradespeople. The focus of envy has been lowered from where it was, on very rich people, to people who are little better-off than the ones who are envious of them. It places the old, the infirm and the unemployed in the dead town centres, and those with 'decent' jobs in the suburbs not far from the new shopping centres where prices are lower.

"Town centres, which are rife with empty, boarded-up shops, close to shoppers at six pm, when gangs of bored teenagers take over the streets. They are not always dangerous, but to many, especially the old, they are intimidating, especially because you can walk the streets for days and never see a police officer… and, since many of these shopping precincts are pedestrianised, police cars cannot patrol them anyway. This has led to the creation of deeper feelings of isolation and demoralisation – as if no-one cares about them or their neighbourhoods any more.

"No wonder there's a feeling of hopelessness in the town and city centres! We ought to go and take a look for ourselves soon. When is everyone available?"

"Any time for me", replied Willy.

"For me too over the next two Earth days", said Becky.

"OK, how about meeting up in twelve Earth hours?" asked Sarah. The others nodded their agreement. "Good, well, let's meet up in twelve hours outside the main gate of Cardiff Castle and we'll take a tour of the four places. We can always go back again at a later date if we feel the need".

∞

"I know that that was only our first quick look around", said Willy, "but it seems to me that Barry has been affected the most out of those four. Not that I used to know the place very well, but you can see that dozens of shops in the town centre are closed awaiting new entrepreneurs. Brecon has fared the best, I think, with the centres of Newport and Cardiff still keeping their heads above water, although when you move out of the central shopping areas, they begin to look more like Barry. Brecon is quite small and still of use to the local community because it is so much closer to the farmers than, say, Cardiff city centre is to its populace. What do you two think?"

"Well, I never have spent much time in any town in South Wales", said Sarah, but the thing that struck me was that there were lots of pawn shops. I doubt if there were so many pawn shops during the Great Depression of the 1930's. And they are in the moderately affluent city centres of Newport and Cardiff, not just in the back streets…"

"And in the centre of Barry…"

"Yes, thank you. I was just about to say that, Becky. They abound where people live… actually live. No-one lives in Queen Street, do they? And you don't find them in the large shopping malls on the outskirts of town either.

"No, people don't travel to sell or pawn their gold, they do it locally, because they are hoping to get it out of hock later".

"Same with second-hand shops… there were loads of them in Barry, and all in the run-down Holton Road area", added Willy. "Did you ever go to Barry much before, Becky?"

"No, not really. Not in town, anyway. John would run us and the kids down to Barry Island a few times in the summer, but I don't remember seeing the town looking as dismal as it does now".

"We never went there often either… We didn't have the time or the transport, but we did go there sometimes, and it was never like it is now. We can check that on the Akashic Record, anyway… I'll do that, I'd find it interesting", said Willy.

"The lack of investment, the lack of money is evident everywhere in all four locations", added Sarah, "as is the closure of religious buildings. There are so many empty or converted churches in all the towns except

Brecon! It is a clear reminder that the Church is not resonating with the youth, although it has probably not done so for fifty years or more".

"At least seventy or eighty, I would say", said Willy. "Yes, eighty or ninety, at least since the The Second World War. In fact, I can't really say that the Church, the organised state churches anyway, ever played a big rôle in my life. Nor in yours, did they, Sarah, so nor in yours either Becky?"

"No, they didn't", mused Becky, "not until after Mum died, anyway. I did give them a try after that for a while…"

"You never mentioned it", said Willy.

"No…" she replied, "I didn't like to".

"I knew though, Becky", said Sarah soothingly, "but it wasn't until you started working with Willy that I could get through to you".

"It's funny, isn't it", asked Willy, "all the major religions prevalent in Europe preach Life After Death, and that Heaven is better than Earth, but very few people, not even the regular church-goers rejoice in the death of a loved one? If Heaven, or Annwn, as we call it locally, is better, why not be happy for someone who goes there? The church commiserates with the loved ones of the dearly departed, but why? Why not just say openly that they should be happy for the deceased? Or the departed, as they say… Departed as in someone going on a journey… perhaps even going home, or at least going on a new adventure".

"The Church just falls in line… they can't afford to alienate their few remaining devotees, perhaps?" asked Becky.

"Maybe", said Sarah ruefully. "The reason why is definitely worth thinking about. "I was talking to some people in one of my classes before we went on our recce today, and one lady and two of her friends had some very interesting observations. They are from a planet called Sinatra. I would like to introduce you to them, if I may". Willy and Becky nodded in agreement.

"Of course, Sarah! That would be great!"

Sarah, closed her eyes for a second, and nodded almost imperceptibly, a smile showed on her lips.

"Hello, Djeesh, thank you for coming to our small meeting. This is Willy, my husband, and this is Becky, our former daughter, but good friend and colleague. Could you introduce us to your friends, please?"

"Certainly, Sarah", said Djeesh without opening her mouth. "These are my friends Ora, and Doram. We are very pleased to meet your friends". A warm 'glow' engulfed the three originally Earthling Spirits, and all six people nodded and smiled at each other. Djeesh and her friends were not from Earth, that much was certain, but Willy was used to meeting 'aliens' because of Sarah's work and studies in the university. He had never met these three people or even this species before, but that was not a problem. They were tall and grey without obvious clothing, but their bodies were ephemeral... ill defined, and there were no obvious signs of their sexuality. Becky put her hands together before her chest in Namaste, as if in prayer, and the Off-Worlders responded in the same way.

Willy and Sarah copied them quickly, smiling broadly.

"Would you like to talk to us, Djeesh? Please feel free to make yourselves comfortable in our apartment according to your custom", said Sarah, sweeping her hand broadly to offer 'the floor' to her guests; then she sat down with her previous family, Willy and Becky, and smiled at her off-world friends in encouragement and anticipation.

"Thank you, Sister Sarah", said Djeesh closing her large eyes momentarily as if to gather her thoughts. Her two friends dropped to the floor and rested on large pillows in the Arab style. "The first thing I want you to be aware of is that my friends and I are communicating at the same time as I am speaking... In the background, you might say. We are pooling our experiences and coming to consensus... and I am voicing that consensus – voicing so to speak". She chuckled shyly at her joke.

"Firstly, we are first-year students from the planet of Sheenatra – sorry to correct you, Sister Sarah. Sinatra was one of your popular singers, I believe". She smiled demurely again.

"We are students on your planet, as you know, and we are studying your People's use of media. You could call it social media, but that is a relatively new term that describes interactive social media, or means of widespread communication. We consider that television, radio and newspapers, including magazines et cetera, are part of this social media However, it suits the powers that be to differentiate between the old style social media and the new, electronic form. This is probably the old classes trying to defend their status as 'professionals', whereas electronic social media is deemed by them to be dominated by amateurs and populists.

"We, my colleagues on my course and I, therefore spend much of our time listening to the radio, watching television and surfing the Internet on your planet. My two friends and I specialise in the United Kingdom of Great Britain and Northern Ireland, which is why we are here – our speciality has a special interest for Sister Sarah, and you, her friends, Sarah says.

"The Internet is still in its early stages here on Earth, and so less irrelevant to your interests, we think. Radio programmes are cheaper to produce than their televisual counterparts, but there is a relevance to your interest, which we will come to later. The most popular social medium by far on this planet is television, although it's popularity is waning amongst the young, who were brought up with the alternative of the Internet providing email, chat rooms, Spotify, and online TV and the like. Older people tend to watch only TV or and listen to the radio, usually Radios Three and Four. This is significant, as we will mention later.

"Television has changed dramatically over the last two decades'", Djeesh was laughing almost uncontrollably behind a hand. "I apologise, but our culture finds puns very funny. Anyway, repeats used to be considered 'bad' in the Seventies, Eighties, Nineties and Noughties, but after that, it became normal to transmit them. Some channels have even made it their raison d'être. It is not unusual to see programmes that are fifty years old. This has never happened before.

"Then, of the new programmes, most of them are of the cheap popular 'Big Brother' type. This reflects popular culture and tighter programming budgets. However, what is interesting, no, you are right,

Brother Ora, very interesting, is that most new dramas in the UK emphasise Great Britain's glorious past, if you consider it glorious. Most television dramas nowadays are about pre-Second World War days… Highlighting the era when Britain ruled the waves and two-thirds of the world. They do not make films or dramas about modern run-down Britain… it is too depressing… It does not highlight the 'Great' part of Great Britain, although 'Great' only ever meant 'Larger' - compared with Brittany, in France.

"This seems to be a concerted effort on behalf of the rich and powerful media tycoons to mask from British people the fact that being part of the European Union was better for them, because it weakened the hold that the British ruling class had over the British people and the British Isles. The televisual multimedia is forcing the British people towards Jingoism and Nationalism by trying to make them pine for the 'Good Old Days of Empire'.

"Excuse me, Sister Djeesh, are you saying that Britain's future is so dismal that the people of Britain are only being shown images of the past?" asked Becky.

"Mmm, not quite, Sister Becky. Britain could have a good future, but only if it is not isolated, and only if it is not exploited. Yes, only if society is fair… -er".

"So, TV dramas are encouraging people towards nationalism in order to isolate them?" asked Willy scratching his head out of habit when he was having trouble comprehending a difficult concept.

"In order to increase nationalism so that leaving the European Union seems more like a good idea, yes. However, that only works with older people. Younger people have no concept of what it was like outside the European Union. The tipping point is that there is a larger number of older people now than at any other era in history. Period dramas are being produced to encourage this large demographic to celebrate having left the European Union".

Djeesh felt a 'Wow' from her British audience and smiled at its acceptance.

"Yes, British people dwell more on and in the past than any other People on the planet of Earth, and that is an obstruction to their progress, and it is being used consciously by certain people to hold the British people back. That is our humble opinion as students looking in, rather than looking out. We are only studying how British people feel. We feel the atmosphere here too, but perhaps not as a Brit would, because of your history and pride in it. We lack that pride in your history".

"Excuse me, Sister Djeesh! I do not want to interrupt your fascinating insights into our culture unnecessarily", said Willy, "but I would like to reassure you that, as an outsider, so to speak, you probably have a clearer, more unbiased viewpoint than most Brits!"

"Thank you, Brother Willy. We appreciate your saying that, and we have to agree".

"There is another aspect that we think is important. Gambling. An abnormally high percentage of television advertisements concerns money. It is perfectly understandable that there are many advertisements concerning money, because they are aimed at the older demographic, which has just come into money from house-price rises, down-sizing, pensions and savings, in a country with an ageing population. However, the profusion of advertisements relating to gambling provides other indications. Wages are low, so the prospect of earning enough money to buy a house, go on holiday or splash out, as you say, is low. This makes for more depression and demoralisation, and gambling. The prospect of getting rich quickly is the only hope some people have. Nevertheless, the hope is fleeting and gambling can easily become addictive, so, in the long run, it tends to have a negative effect on the participants.

"In summation, many, too many, of new television programmes look back to what is perceived as a 'glorious' past, whilst for many, the only real hope for a prosperous future is gambling. In this situation, it appears to us that most British people have a dim view of their future, which, because of their pride in their history, leads many to lay the blame elsewhere. Foreigners are the obvious people to blame - foreigners of colour are the easiest group to distinguish. Therefore, xenophobia is often the result. A particular manifestation of this xenophobia in the United Kingdom is Brexit, but it would have outed itself in another way sooner or later because of the forces of frustration and demoralisation pent up in the population.

"The danger is that, if Brexit does not lead to increased prosperity, the British people will have no-one left to blame and civil disobedience and eventually unrest will inevitably be the result

"This is our combined conclusion".

"You do not paint a very happy future for the British people, my friends", said Sarah. "However, we thank you for being frank with us in sharing the results of your study. I know that you have another appointment soon, so, on behalf of my 'family', I would like to thank you again for your time and input. I'll see you all in school tomorrow. Goodbye for now".

After they had left, Sarah said, "So there you have it. The indication from an outside perspective is one of increased social depression and demoralisation, which is manifesting itself in increased gambling, frequent period dramas and xenophobia. The future looks bleak, and could lead to civil unrest, which could conceivably bring about government reprisals and a martial state, resulting in reduced civil liberty, and more national unhappiness, which would justify more repression, and an ever-worsening downward spiral. Where that could lead is anyone's guess, but there is a good chance that the future for the UK is bleak.

"Do either of you have any observations?"

The three friends sat looking at each other and the floor as they fell into their own analyses of Britain's future.

"I have one more point to make", said Becky. "I noticed that far more people are using recreational drugs and alcohol far more than they used to. For example, when I was growing up, Dad was the only one in the house who drank and that was only in the pub. He would go to the village pub two or three times a week, and never brought the habit back home. You never drank, Mam, and I didn't drink or smoke either, like you.

"However, nowadays, people of all ages drink and smoke and are proud of it. I see my children, my grandchildren and their friends drinking and taking drugs all the time, and they think nothing of it. If you ask someone whether they had a good time at a party or night out, it is quite unremarkable to get the reply: 'Fantastic! Everyone was really out of it!'. You or Dad would never have given a reply like that. Being 'out of control' was not something to boast about – quite the contrary – but these days it is something people are proud of. That is a huge change in social attitudes in one generation".

"That is a good point, Becky. That also points towards instant gratification – like gambling. A quick fix, instant happiness, which is short-lived, and ultimately depressing when the hit is over. So, that pretty much sums up the situation, I think. The problem that faces us, if we want to help, is how we can provide that assistance… What can we do?"

4. Becky Past and Present

While Willy was on The Surface, Becky had learned a great deal about how the Universe worked through her interaction with her father, and the leaders of a nearby Spiritualist Church, Gareth and Emma, but when he passed away, things had begun to go downhill for her. John, her husband had been the first to give up on her. Their marriage had been pretty rocky for some time, but when John felt that she was spending too much time at the church in one Circle or another, he began to seek comfort elsewhere. By this time, her children were of university age and they couldn't wait to leave the shell of a building, which they had previously referred to as a loving home.

Becky had taken to drink again, as she had when her father had died, but no amount of comforting from her parents had been enough to help her shed the depression she felt. She had managed to eke out an existence for almost a decade, not that she was short of money, but she had finally contracted sclerosis of the liver and died a little over a year later. She had been only forty-six years of age, and people mourned that she had died 'too young', in the prime of her life.

She had seemed to forget that there were people on Earth who cared for her, but they were there at her funeral. Little did many of them realise that Becky had planned to 'die' long before she was born, so that she could return to Annwn when her work on Earth was complete. She had returned to the loving arms of her parents, who were her parents no longer, although it was difficult to get out of the habit of a lifetime, so she still referred to them as Mam and Dad sometimes.

Relationships and feelings of close love for friends from lives before her latest with Willy and Sarah had long since dissipated. Not that they were lost and gone forever, it was just that people forged so many friendships during a lifetime on The Surface, or on whichever planet that they happened to be, and there were so many lifetimes, that keeping in touch with anyone 'from previously' was difficult. She knew that her children didn't miss her much. She hadn't really been there for them in the last decade of her life, but then by then, they had learned to do without her… and their father, because John had moved on even before Becky had 'abandoned' them. He was now happy with his younger wife and her children, who were too young to ask for too much of his money. Becky no longer had any interest in or communication with John whatsoever. She still loved her children though and took an active interest in what they were doing. She knew exactly what their life's aspirations were, she had discussed them with them before they had been born to her and John. They had wandered off track a little, but not irreversibly so, and she was confident that they would get there in the end with a few friendly, maternal nudges from her. Eventually, they would become part of her team on Earth, as planned. First joining one of her existing Development Circles and eventually forming their own, which, because they had such a strong filial bond with one another, would become a real force for Enlightenment, Truth and Change - a genuine, permanent change which would start a new movement for equality for all.

She knew that South Wales had a bright future, although not necessarily a prosperous one. However, it would be a fairer place to live than almost anywhere else on Earth as it had been about a hundred years before when free health care at the point of delivery and a fledgling social security service had been established by local residents without any help or encouragement from the government, and near universal resistance from the doctors and their associations like the British Medical Association.

It was time for the next Big Push in society, and she could not only see it coming, but she was determined to be an integral part of it from planning to implementation, and so were most of her recent family and close friends.

And she couldn't wait, although she knew that she would have to - it just wasn't one of her strong points.

Becky was a kind-hearted soul. She, like Willy and Sarah, had lived many lives, more than she could remember, most of them on Earth, but not all. For Earth was a lower to-intermediary world of education. There were some lower, but most were superior. She and her friends could have moved on, if they had wanted to, their vibrations were just about high enough, but they had all chosen to work as a group to help raise the frequency of the inhabitants of the planet; to help improve the quality of the lessons that could be learned there. Their goal was to raise the bar.

Souls with lower vibrations would always need to be able to go somewhere, if they decided that they wanted to continue their education, but there would always be enough environments for them. Becky wanted to improve her school with the passion of an Old Girl, who had done well and wanted to join the Board of Governors to repay some of the debt she thought she owed the school and its past masters. In truth, this was her all-consuming passion of the day. Sure, she loved her latest brood of children, but in the manner that a Sire and Bitch might love the off-spring they are with, their latest brood, until those puppies went out into the world and tried to make it on their own, or until it was time to lead the next life and the next brood was born.

This was the way things worked. It was not callous or cold-hearted, for how could someone love and take an active interest in all the children one may have over tens of millennia or longer? Thousands of children, many of whom could be older and wiser than oneself in the Spiritual sense? No, her real passion was not her immediate 'family', but helping to facilitate the eternal progression of all those who desired it, and that meant, in her eyes, the improvement of the school.

The way that she chose to bring this about was to show those who could not remember – the overwhelming majority – that there was Life After Death, Reincarnation, and Karma, and that Karma would ensure that everyone got their just rewards or penalty for their action whilst incarnate. Her hope was that if more people realised that they cannot ever get away with obstructing others, then they would only try to help instead, thus increasing the enjoyment of life on The Surface almost instantaneously.

However, it was not that easy in practise. Trying to teach three-year-olds quadratic equations is tough, almost pointless, yet not quite impossible, because some did get it; they just needed reminding, and this was the point of Becky's Development Circles. She was passionate about her Spiritual Development Circles, which were almost exclusively connected to Spiritualist Churches. The dozen or so members of the Circle would learn about psychic phenomena, and then perhaps give demonstrations of their abilities, which would hopefully persuade others that Life After Death and Karma really did exist.

Little by little, Becky and those like her were raising Mankind's ability to perceive the whole world and not just the part that is normally perceptible to an average human being through the five senses that material scientists agree on.

Becky was much more aware of what was going on on The Surface than the average resident of Annwn too – far more than Willy, though not Sarah – because of her participation in her Circles. She talked to all sorts of people from all walks of life every day. The members were very diverse in nature: not all of one sex, not all old, not all poor or wealthy, not all of one class, religion or education, and they brought with them a rich feedback in their weekly discussions.

She knew that of the four municipalities that they had chosen to study, by far the most affected by modern affairs was Barry. All four areas had undergone adverse change brought about by the Austerity measures and pandemic of late, but Cardiff and Newport were large enough to still provide entertainment for people of all ages, and work of some kind to most of those who sought it, although the wages were lower in real terms than they had been decades before. Housing was less of a problem too. Although the cost of buying a house was out of most people's reach, there were plenty of apartments and student studio flats for rent, although the cost was high.

Brecon had also been affected, but being situated in the middle of what was mostly a farming community, it suffered less. Kids could live at home, if necessary. Housing for the young had always been a problem, it was nothing new. Likewise with employment. If someone didn't want to follow on into the family farm, then Cardiff was not far away, and neither was Newport. Brecon had been most affected by a drop in the number of visitors and holiday-makers, as the holiday-making population of the UK felt the pinch and the lock-down. The highlight of the social calendar was, and had been for decades, the Brecon Jazz Festival for which accommodation had to be booked up at least a year in advance, especially at the plusher venues like The Castle Hotel overlooking the village, although that too had been cancelled because of the virus in recent years.

However, Barry was different. Barry had been a thriving town in the memories of many of its citizens. The docks, before the War, had been so busy that it was possible to cross them by walking from deck to deck. Ships from all over the world had taken coal away from The Valleys, and brought pit-props and bananas amongst other goods in. The docks had been a major employer paying good wages, as had the chemical plants on the southern outskirts of the town. Barry Island had been famous for its beaches, fair ground and the Pelican Night Club run by the Morgan family, which sailors had known about the world over. Butlin's Holiday Camp had brought in three thousand visitors a week, and guest houses were normally full all summer long. People over the age of fifty recounted with passionate nostalgia memories of happy days on the beach or at the Knap Lido – a 120 by 30 yard outdoor swimming pool. The pool was long gone, and few people used the beaches now because of pollution from sewage dumped as 'overspill' by the water authority, which meant that the fairground was suffering. A fairground that had employed many young people throughout the long summer school holidays, as had the holiday camp.

All gone and not replaced, which meant that the youth of the town had no work and no money. Their parents could not help as they were also suffering from the massively damaging downturn in work, and the amount of social security benefits, always low, had been frozen for years, while inflation continued to push up prices. This sad state of affairs had the knock-on effects usually associated with it.

The top quality restaurants of Barry's past were now shut and gone forever, and half of Barry's bars and working-men's clubs had closed down, because their previous clientèle could no longer afford to patronise them. Many of those that remained looked tired and worn. Shopping was even worse. Most women complained that if they wanted to buy 'something nice', they had to go into Cardiff, and it was true. The high street in town, called Holton Road, was a shadow of its former self. The only clothes shop sold cheap clothing to suit the impecunious residents who used the area, Second-hand shops, pawn shops and gambling joints proliferated. Many potential sales outlets were boarded up, and two of the town centre's three pubs were no more. One was boarded up with a homeless man sleeping permanently in the shelter he had constructed in its doorway, and the other was a mini supermarket. Yet both had been popular venues only a few decades before providing food and drink to hundreds of lunchtime shoppers and near-by workers.

They represented stark evidence of how quickly and how far the town of Barry had fallen.

Barry had become a suburb of Cardiff, and both the elderly and the young resented the downgrade. Barry was easily the most demoralised and depressed town in the area, and the most surprising aspect was that crime levels had not soared far higher than they were already. In the town centre, it was as if the inhabitants 'were all in it together'. They were all facing hard times, so thieves and burglars left them alone.

It seemed that many, if not most of the active residents in the inner town centre had a black job, or 'fiddle' on the side. In order to make their money up to a liveable wage. Some resold foreign tobacco, which bore far less tax, imported by smugglers; some produced and sold home-made wine; others sold flowers or vegetables from their gardens or allotments; and yet others carried out home repairs, tidied gardens, took dogs for walks, babysat or repaired clothing. Ironically, the device that had caused the downfall of so many inner cities, the Internet, was also being used as a sideline to sell goods on eBay, and the many more local clones of it.

Drugs were the worst result of the depression, shortage of money and lack of local entertainment. Most residents were not touched by the underground drug sub-culture of the town, but too many were. However, many young adults, teenagers and even children were involved, and that affected their parents, friends and family. Older drug dealers had discovered that children made ideal mules to deliver their recreational drugs, as the few police officers left working in the town were not looking for them. They exploited the children ruthlessly, and the kids felt like royalty with the extra money they were paid.

Jealousy had quickly ensued, which had soon led to rival gangs fighting turf wars, and that had forced many young people to carry knives to defend themselves, guns not being readily available to children in the UK at that point in history. Often, the mules would take the drugs themselves and this sometimes led to personal grievances being settled with a knife fight. Children were dying of knife wounds every week in and around Barry. There had been an increase in muggings too, but it was not as severe as the rise in stabbings among young adults and children. Even children not involved with drugs felt they had to carry a knife in order to protect themselves from the crazy kids who did carry them, since there were not enough police officers on the streets to protect them.

Becky had been sadly moved by three stories she had heard that very week from individuals at a Circle she frequently attended in Butrill's Road Spiritualist Church.

The first had been related by a young man of twenty years, Lewis, who had already lost three close friends to drug violence in his short life. Two had been murdered in knife fights and one had committed suicide. His everyday life was fraught with fear that he might be next, although he had nothing to do with the drug culture. For the sake of safety, he never went out alone – always with a few friends – and they all felt that they had to carry knives in case they were attacked. He had said that he expected to be involved in a serious, perhaps fatal, knife fight within a year.

The second had been told by an older man. He had been sitting on a bench watching shoppers passing by while catching his breath, when a young man walked rapidly past him and collided with a tree. He had hit the tree with his nose and forehead at about four or five miles an hour. His nose had exploded, and he had taken two steps back before walking into the tree again. The young female teenager sitting near him had said: "People just don't realise how strong Spice is", and the boy had marched off, nose steaming with blood watched by half a dozen shocked shoppers. He then walked into the large, clear glass window of a superstore opposite. A lady had gone to help him, but she had only pointed him to the left and he had marched off in that direction. "That woman was lucky", said the teenage girl. "I wouldn't have helped him. He might have been carrying a knife and taken offence, if he thought that people were laughing at him. You have to be very careful…"

The third had been told by a woman who had also been shopping in the town centre and taken a rest in a pub there.

"We had only been back in Barry, my home town for six months" she had said, "but it didn't take that long to realise that there were street problems that were unusual. At least, I wasn't used to them, but then, of the previous fifteen years, I had spent thirteen in Thailand and two in Spain. One of the first things that my husband and I noticed was the lack of a police presence on the streets. The second was the deserted streets after dark - a sign that suggested to us that the unsavoury ruled the streets during that period.

"One afternoon, a friend, who seems to know a lot, told me that the night before, there had been only two police cars on duty in Barry - a town of 60,000 inhabitants. The lack of a visible police presence was beginning to make sense.

"A few days later", she had continued, "a man, whom I also know well, told me that he had spent the last hour with an elderly lady, who had fallen over and cracked her head on the pavement. My friend had phoned the emergency services, but it had still taken an hour for them to arrive.

"And then, just before Christmas, I was sitting in a pub opposite a local supermarket" she continued, "when a woman started to beat a young boy. He was six, seven, eight years of age. One of the men in the pub sprinted out to reprimand her, but the mother had already disappeared inside to do her shopping, leaving the boy crying in a huddle in a corner.

"He had phoned the police, comforted the boy and returned inside to watch what would happen. When the boy ran off, the caller got cold feet and left, but the police never arrived, and the woman emerged from the shop and called a taxi. The police did not show up at all.

"That is my experience of modern Barry - it has changed so much since I last lived here".

Barry was unusual though, in that none of the bars in the centre tolerated drugs at all. Most towns had bars where the discreet smoking of marijuana in the garden by locals was overlooked by the landlord. However, this was not the case in the four bars remaining on the entire length of Holton Road: The Tadross Hotel, O'Briens, The Buck and The Butterfly Collector.

The youth drank and smoked drugs in the parks, and the adults smoked at home, but drank in the pubs as well as in the house. Open street violence among adults was rare, since vicinities and bars policed themselves. People who were experiencing difficulties with someone were more likely to go to a local tough guy than the police. The clock had been turned back to the days of the mafia – the Kray Twins and the Richardson's.

Becky had lived many lives in many different ages and knew that people had long taken drugs for two main reasons: the first was to seek enlightenment and the second to forget their worldly problems.

The Hippies of the Seventies had sought enlightenment, but it seemed from having listened to Lewis that no-one did it for that reason any longer. He had explained that he had seen his friends' grandparents and parents taking drugs all his life and that no-one had ever said that they were looking for knowledge. As far as he was concerned, people only took drugs because they were cheaper than alcohol and they only took both or either of them to forget the problems that they had such as lack of money, lack of security and lack of meaningful, well-paid work.

It was a depressing thought for Becky, and her disappointment was obvious in her Aura as she related her findings to Willy and Sarah at one of their regular meetings.

"It is sad, really sad, and depressing, that is for certain", said Willy. "It makes the task we have set ourselves look rather hopeless, doesn't it?"

"It will be a long-term operation, yes, and probably take longer than we first thought", opined Sarah. "It is a real shame, and we will probably need help. I think we ought to pay Steven another visit soon".

"Do you mind if I ask my Spirit Guide, Huw, to come here for a moment, if he has the time?"

"No, not at all", answered Sarah, looking at Willy for confirmation, which he gave with a shrug and a smile. "I like Huw, he's a very knowledgeable person, and expresses himself very clearly".

"I agree", said Willy. "It would be lovely to see him again".

Becky was silent for a couple of seconds… a little distant in her demeanour, and then Huw was standing amongst them. People put their hands together in the typical Buddhist greeting that the Indians call Namaste and the Thais call a Waai.

After the welcome, Becky offered Huw a seat and everyone sat down to talk.

"We have been talking about how to raise the amount of good feeling in Barry and the South Wales area. I have mentioned this to you before, Huw, but would you give us your views on the matter, please?"

"Of course, Becky. I am honoured that you seek my opinion. OK, for what it is worth, I think that your tactic of using Spiritualist Churches to promote the concepts of Life After Death, Reincarnation and Karma is the correct one", said their close friend and Becky's current Spirit Guide, Huw. "When my last parents were living on The Surface, they helped run Psychic Development Circles in the Barry area, the purpose of which was exactly the same as yours. They saw a lot of success".

"Well, that's good news, isn't it, Sarah? Willy?" asked Becky.

"Yes, most encouraging!" said Willy.

"Of course, a belief in Karma is what clinches it, wouldn't you say, Huw?" asked Sarah.

"Yes, but the three concepts are inextricably entwined, aren't they? Just believing in Karma is not a deterrent to bad behaviour, if there is no Life After Death, or at least, not so much of one for an old person, since Karma is suspended in Annwn. No-one can hurt anyone here, so it is impossible to rack up or dissipate bad Karma here. The bad Karma will only affect your next lifetime, so for Karma to be an effective deterrent to bad deeds, then you have to establish a Life After Death and subsequent Reincarnation, during which time the evil-doer will get his or her comeuppance".

"Yes, I can see that, Huw. It is a package – a trilogy of concepts - or it is nothing".

"Yes, I would say so, Sarah. Do you have any specific plans in mind?" asked Huw.

"Well, 'Yes and 'No', I think…" replied Sarah looking to the others for help. "That is, we had very vague plans… or let's say that we, Willy and I noticed one night while walking through the centre of Cardiff, how many people were sleeping rough, and we thought that we would like to try to do something about it. In fact, it was Willy's idea really…"

"OK", Willy picked up. "like a bull at a gate, I thought that I would be reincarnated as soon as possible to see what I could do to alleviate the situation. However, it soon became obvious to me that, on my own, there was little that I could do. I could see that Sarah wanted to help… and that was great. Anyway, we took the idea to Becky, who was already aware of the problem and the three of us put our heads together. We think, that the situation in South Wales, or even Britain as a whole, and possibly the whole world, is only going to get worse, and that is not something that we want to see without doing all we can to help. Right, guys?" They both smiled and nodded.

"Admirable sentiments, but have you considered that the way things are working out on The Surface was planned so that people could have the chance of experiencing them?"

The three friends looked at each other stony-faced.

"All right", said Huw sensing that they had come to an impasse, "I think that it is a good idea if I leave you with that thought. However, if you ever want to talk to me again, about this or anything else, please do not hesitate to contact me either directly or through Becky. Thank you for inviting me". Huw smiled, Waaied and disappeared.

"Well, that was, er, interesting", said Willy. "and he is right, of course. The situation that so worries us, could have been brought about on purpose in order to offer new experiences, er, new courses. So, what do we do now?"

"I suggest that we continue as planned and visit Steven, but all the while considering what Huw has just said", suggested Sarah. "What do you reckon, Becky?"

"I agree, Mam. Dad?"

"Yes, I agree too".

5. Karma

The Immutable Law of Reciprocation

"Well, the Holocaust is a mute philosophical question on Earth, of course", said Stephen in one of the rooms in the University of Annwn in the city of Annwn. "People on The Surface do not always say what they mean or mean what they say. This often has to do with convention, but also fear of reprisals from someone, or some group, more powerful, irrespective of who is right or who is wrong. We in Annwn do not have those problems to worry about, since no-one can cause us any physical harm here. Shirley MacLaine had no end of bad press because it was reported that she had said that the Jews had brought the Holocaust upon themselves through bad Karma, or even through their own choice. You can look up what she actually said on the Akashic Record, but it is true that anyone who ever suffers on Earth has done so either through Karma or their own volition. That is through choosing a course of study that involved physical injury or the threat of it. However, more often than not, Karma will wreak its revenge through mental anguish.

"I suspect that this is what Miss MacLaine was alluding to, but she didn't ever really get the chance to explain herself. It is one of the problems of being incarnate, societies have their customs and taboos, so there are some things that one just cannot say yet. The thought police will not allow it, because it does not fit their agenda, and most people and all Peoples have an agenda. We don't suffer from that restriction in Annwn, which makes discussion easier. As I said, the phenomenon is not uncommon throughout the Universe, but prejudice and hypocrisy are strong on Earth because so many people are only interested in advancing their own aims, which all too often means themselves, and their own bank balances. Greed, fanned by personal ambition, is a prominent feature of life on this planet.

"Greed, the desire for money, is the most common reason for retribution by Karma here".

"So, is greed the reason for the current state of affairs in Wales and the UK as a whole, Steven?" asked Willy.

"Yes, Willy. However, just to finish my earlier point, the case of Miss MacLaine is a good example of what can result from telling the truth on The Surface. However, knowing that here and remembering it after you have been reborn are two quite separate things… and, of course, times change. What the people in your 'company' allow people to say varies… it also changes over time. To quote a recent trend, 'political correctness' is a mutating philosophy. It is well to keep up with the trend or risk the consequences, which vary from ridicule, through verbal abuse to actual bodily harm or even murder".

"Yes, that was the way things were heading when I left. It's worse now, is it?" asked Willy.

"Yes. I'm afraid so. In fact, as far as the lives of average people go, most aspects of their lives have worsened. From our point of view though, more people than for a long time are seeking answers in the traditional ways. I don't mean state-organised religions either. People are leap-frogging that era and going back to the pre-Christian era. They are looking back to the time before the state corrupted religion for its own ends, which was what Christ and Mohammed were also trying to achieve, ironically… Buddha and many others too, I might add", replied Steven.

"Well, before we get onto that, Willy, I know that you are impatient to get to the heart of the matter, I just want to add that all the vices that could trigger Karma can and almost always do have an adverse effect on the health of the physical body. Some say that this is Karma at work, others say that it is a result of leading a stressful life of lies and deceit, and yet others say that it is the physical world's way of cleansing itself of poor quality inhabitants! In truth, it doesn't matter which way that you look at it, because the result is the same.

"At this point, I think it is important to draw this distinction: not everyone who dies young or in pain does so because of bad Karma. It is simply one of the reasons – and far from the most common".

"What are the others then, please, Steven? "asked Becky, warming to the subject.

"Well, there are cases where a Soul has chosen a way of life, what you might call a course… like a university degree course, and bites off more than he can chew, as they say so eloquently in the English language. In other words, despite all the help, advice and counselling one can get in Annwn, he is unable to complete the course because it brings on too much suffering, and terminates his study prematurely by committing suicide. This is against the rules because courses on Earth, well, anywhere really, are limited in number, so suicide brings a penalty - a punishment, if you like. The Soul in question is not allowed to take another course, until he has lived out the full number of years he should have lived in the life before. For example, if the course is programmed to last, say, fifty years, and the Soul kills himself at forty-five, then he has to return to live out the shortfall or remaining five years, which will obviously be as a child that 'dies young'.

"This might not sound much of a hardship, but it involves finding parents who will help; dying again; and having to be reborn just to pick up where he left off. It can, and usually does, mean a massive waste of time for the one who committed suicide, while not burdening the parents in the child's short life because it is part of their course. In such cases, the ones one has to feel sorry for are those who were relying on him to complete his course so that they could complete theirs…"

"What happens to them? "asked Becky.

"Well, they do literally lose out, which is why suicide is such a 'sin'… It is a sin against one's fellows, not against God as people would have you believe. God doesn't care, but your schoolmates certainly do! It's like not turning up for a sports match, when you have been picked to be in the team. It is one of those many instances where people say the right thing but for the wrong reason by blaming God for getting upset. It is quite funny, isn't it, to think that whatever one calls God worries about whether you drop out of a course! Would the Prime Minister care if you dropped out of your biology course at Portsmouth University? It is ridiculous!"

"Another might be to help his team. For example, a child might die in pain to serve several purposes. One could be to draw attention to a problem in society - say, a shortage of local healthcare due to Austerity, which could be due to greed; or to help his 'family' be strong in the face of adversity, or just to overcome grief. There are many, many reasons why someone might die what by-standers, or even team members think is young. It is rarely the case that a child dies at a young age because it cannot cope with the course it has chosen. This is another example of ignorant people jumping to the wrong conclusion either because they don't understand death and are grieving, or because they are frightened of death and are worried about it.*.

"It seems that humans have forgotten a lot", said Willy sadly.

"Actually, it depends what you mean, Willy. While it is true that the memories of most Souls are wiped clean at birth, some didn't know much to have wiped in the first place. An advanced Soul will probably know very little in his early life on Earth, say, but he will be easy to teach, because his memories may return either wholly or in part. By the way, this has nothing to do with Karma. However, there are Souls who have been, let's say, lazy, and not made full use of their existence to study. They will obviously have less to forget at birth and subsequently remember. The opposite will be true of an industrious person. Do you see what I mean? Yes, I am sure that you do. Although all Souls were created at the same time and equal, some have chosen to progress while others have not.

"Please note well, that this is not the same as on The Surface, where all people, and Peoples, are not born equal and not given an equal chance to succeed - no matter what the ruling classes of unfair societies say!"

"I hope that that short resume of the meaning of Karma didn't bore you, but it is important that we are talking about the same thing when we use the word Karma. On The Surface, so many people use different interpretations of the word. And there is more to the concept than I have outlined here, but our examples are sufficient to define the term accurately enough for our current purposes. Are there any questions?"

"Are there any exceptions to the Law of Karma?" asked Willy. "I mean, children cannot be expected to know about it, and so might transgress its laws without knowing".

"No, there are no exceptions to the Law of Karma. Never, never, ever. At rebirth on The Surface, even the most experienced Souls - Jesus, Mohammed, Buddha and all the rest – were all born babies. How can exceptions be made?

"So, getting back to your case in hand, I am not trying to discourage you from returning to The Surface as bodhisattvas. Don't think that. Millions of people have tried what you are contemplating... the big three, Buddha, Christ and Mohammed, just became more famous because they were backed by the ruling classes, when they realised that they couldn't beat them. The overwhelming majority of bodhisattvas slip into obscurity, not that fame was their intention anyway.

"So, what I am trying to say is that obscurity does not equal failure. It would be a serious mistake to think that. Every effort, whether it carries the movement forward a mile or a step, is progress, isn't it? A step in the right direction, so to speak...". Steven looked at his audience, and saw by their smiles that they understood.

"We were thinking more of a triad", said Sarah. "The three of us working together, but we are not sure about how to use us in the best way. Perhaps, Willy and I could be close relatives and Becky a cousin... or maybe she should stay here and co-ordinate...?"

"Nobody has ever worked alone, as far as that goes, Sarah".

"No, of course not, Steven. This is our first attempt at such a mission, and it is a lot to take in... and even harder to remember. So, we might as well all go..."

"It really is completely up to you. You would potentially gain more traction if the three of you were working from three separate families".

The three once-related friends silently agreed. "Thank you, Steven. You have been extremely helpful", said Becky. They all nodded in agreement, waaied, and disappeared.

∞

At a meeting to discuss how to proceed with their idea to help the South Wales area, Willy received a message that startled him.

"I'm really sorry, my friends, but I have just been made aware of another shocking case of animal cruelty. It is very distressing… It involves an endangered species too. I just can't believe it! So many people have been… are, working so hard to stamp this insane barbarism out… Barbarians wouldn't even stoop this low. They would know that you have to manage… maintain the stock. These people are just out for what they can get right now, and don't give two hoots about tomorrow.

"I just can't believe it!" Willy repeated.

"What is upsetting you so, my darling?" asked Sarah.

"I don't know how much either of you know about the Siberian tiger?"

"Something", replied Sarah.

"Yes, one of the largest cats in the world… endangered, I should think", added Becky. "They didn't feature much on our little mountain, did they?"

"No", replied Willy, "they didn't, and just as well, I suppose. They would have eaten our sheep, and there would have been only two options: capture or kill. Unfortunately, it is easier to kill them than capture them. Anyway, I have just received a message from someone I know called Vikki She has a soft spot for Siberian tigers. She has contacts in some areas where they live, and has worked for decades to increase their numbers, and prevent their slaughter for the so-called health industry in Asia, and specifically, China.

"Well, since Vikki and I became friends, and that was specifically to do with the Siberian tiger, which is scientifically known as Panthera tigris altaica, I have made a study… more like a hobby of them too. A Siberian is huge! It stands as one of the most majestic and enigmatic creatures on Earth. You have to try this one time - stand up close to one! They are endowed with awe-inspiring strength, breathtaking agility, and an unmistakable aura of regality! This magnificent big cat roams the expansive landscapes of the Russian Far East and parts of northeastern China. Unfortunately, that's where my news is about.

Becky quoted an unseen source aloud:

"'The Siberian tiger is an embodiment of feline power and grace. Among the largest of large cats, it boasts a robust build, with males weighing up to a staggering eight hundred pounds and stretching over ten feet in length, tail included. Its coat, a striking combination of golden-orange and white, is accentuated by characteristic black stripes that serve as nature's signature adornment. This fur provides vital insulation against the frigid temperatures of its native terrain, ensuring it thrives even in the most unforgiving winters'.

"Again, unfortunately, therefrom stems the reason for its rapid demise. People in those parts of the world think that if they eat this animal, they will be endowed with its prowess. Not only that, but men like to prove their valour by killing them, and people of both sexes like to wear their skins to keep warm!" said Willy.

"It makes my blood boil… well, it would, if I still had any…", he joked, trying to be less serious, but failing.

Becky quoted further:

"'The Siberian tiger is profoundly linked to the vast taiga, a biome of immense coniferous forests, sprawling across Siberia. Here, amid the towering pines and dense undergrowth, the tiger finds its fortress. The taiga offers an abundance of prey, such as deer, boar, and elk, ensuring sustenance for these apex predators. Rivers, lakes, and marshes provide vital water sources while offering prime ambush sites for hunting. This biologically diverse environment fosters a delicate ecological balance, of which the Siberian tiger is both steward and sentinel. It is also very difficult for man to hunt them down. The Siberian Tiger has a good chance of survival here, but the same cannot be said for those that wander into China"'.

"In the middle of the 20th Century, there could have been as few as twenty left. Now, it is estimated that there are about 600, but it is not enough to ensure their survival as a species. It's not only rampant poaching that's to blame though, man is also encroaching on its habitat in the search for minerals" added Willy

"It's a crying shame, it really is!" Willy fell silent, and his friends reached out to comfort him.

"I have to go there now to offer my help…" said Willy after a few moments.

"Of course you do, my dear, and we're coming with you, aren't we, Becky?" replied Sarah.

"Yes, if we won't be in the way".

"Of course, you're both welcome, most welcome to come too. I'd like you to very much, in fact".

"That's settled then", said Sarah smiling. "Just say the magic word", she joked.

"Shazam!" shouted Willy smiling for the first time in a while, and the three friends disappeared from the room above the sanctuary and appeared on the shore of a vast expanse of water.

"It is so beautiful!" exclaimed Becky, "Where are we?"

"We are standing on the shore of the Heavenly Lake on, or should I say, in Paektu Mountain (in Korean) or Changbai Mountain (in Chinese) just to the north of the Chinese / North Korean border at about 2,744m above sea level. It's a stratovolcano, and the tallest mountain in the Changbai or Paektu Mountain Range… It's part of the Siberian Tiger's range too. Although they call it the Amur Tiger in these parts. The lake lies in its caldera, and it's held sacred by the indigenous people. It, the caldera, was formed in 946 AD, when the volcano erupted casting more than a hundred cubic kilometres of tephra into the skies. It was one of the biggest eruptions in the last five thousand years. It last blew its top in 1903, and people are saying that another one is due soon. There are scientific observation posts dotted about measuring seismic activity… Just to be fair, I ought to say that this is a nature reserve, and there are wardens protecting the Siberian Tigers too.

"If you had a body, you'd probably be dead by now dressed like that", he joked. He was feeling happier now that he had taken some kind of positive action. "Despite the lake being up to three hundred and eighty-four metres deep, it is frozen over for ten months of the year. The names for the mountain all refer to it being eternally white with snow, and the temperature goes as low as -50c, although the average is only -4.9c… let's call it -5c just between us, and the average wind speed is 42 kph. You've got to be tough to live around here!

"Our tigers are just that, but they weren't designed to fight against greedy cowards with traps and long-range rifles. My boiling blood would keep me warm up here, if I were still incarnate". Sarah and Becky shared a pensive glance during his tirade, justified though they thought it was.

"So, what's our next move, Dad?" asked Becky. She still found it difficult to call him Willy or even William.

"My friend Vikki is at work now - at her desk in Barry, as it happens - but she has told me to meet a local woman called Chen Mei here. Mei is her first name, by the way". They looked around themselves, and Becky pointed out over the lake. A silver globe, or star shape, was speeding towards them, growing larger, but not brighter, at about two metres above the water, although there was no reflection on the water. The light stopped about three metres from them, and a woman appeared. She seemed to be Asian and in her mid-twenties with hair hanging down to her waist. She waaied, smiled and advanced to the group.

"Hello", she said, "you must be Willy. Nice to meet you and your friends. My name is Chen Mei. Please call me Mei. You are just as Vikki described you, Willy". He wasn't sure what that meant, but he felt a little embarrassed, so quickly introduced his 'family'.

"We are only here as observers, and thank you for allowing us to come. Thank you for calling in the first place even. It is such an honour". He was gushing, and knew it. He was feeling attracted to the young woman, and felt guilty about it.

"Not at all. It is we who should feel honoured that you take an interest in our local affairs. Please allow me to brief you on the situation so far. Let us sit on these rocks near the shoreline". Mei put a hand out to guide Willy, and he did the same for Sarah, who could not help finding Willy's embarrassment amusing. She and Becky were almost giggling.

Once seated, Mei began to speak. "As you become more familiar with the area, you will notice a lot of soldiers, both Chinese and Korean. You will not see so many of our beloved Amur tigers. You call them Siberian, that is the Russian name. I know that you already know a great deal about these magnificent cats, Willy - Vikki told me. Have you appraised your colleagues?" He assured her that he had with only barely looking at her. Mei was beginning to notice his feelings in his Aura and smiled knowingly at Sarah, who felt neither animosity nor jealousy.

"In the old days, the tiger had more of a chance against poachers, but now, with surveillance cameras, drones, mobile phones and high-powered hunting rifles, the cats don't really stand a chance… a cat in Hell's chance, eh?" Sarah and Becky smiled at Mei's joke, but Willy could not look at her for fear of 'blushing'. His predicament added to the ladies' amusement as he squirmed in uncomfortable embarrassment.

"Sometimes, the soldiers will kill an Amur if it crosses their path, but this is rare. They are more likely to accept bribes from the poachers from China and Korea to look the other way, while they carry out their illegal activity. This is what is happening not far from here. If you are ready, I can take you there now. Please follow me. Willy? Are you ready?" Mei held out a hand to him, and the three women giggled under their breath.

"It's all right, Willy. Everybody knows that you find Mei attractive", said Sarah in a private thought. "It's not something that you can hide from people like us, is it? It is also perfectly normal. She is a beautiful, charming woman. It would be very strange if you didn't like her, so stop behaving like a sixteen-year-old with a crush, and act like a grown-up. You are not upsetting me. Just be yourself. You're a good man, so just behave normally".

"You're right," he replied sheepishly. "I just thought… well, maybe thought is the wrong word under the circumstances, but I just didn't want to hurt you".

"You haven't, and you won't. Don't worry".

"Thank you, my dear. I can be such a clown sometimes, can't I?"

"It is one of the characteristics that makes you so adorable, and I am proud that Mei likes you. Just act normal… Be yourself".

Willy stepped forward towards Mei smiling. She dropped the arm that she had held out for him with a smile, pointed to the east and said, "Follow me!"

Leaving Annwn

6. Freedom Beckons

The four friends drifted up the east wall of the caldera, and then plunged over the top in a wide arc which took them south-south-east. They came to Earth amid a pile of boulders about five hundred metres above level ground.

"I didn't take you directly into the camp, because some of them can see our orbs as we travel. They have seen so many that they are quite used to them now, but we are not sure whether any of them are psychic. Anyway, we won't have aroused any suspicion… more like superstition!" Mei laughed at her own joke. You see, many of the people living around this mountain believe that it is where they came from… and they are not far wrong. A lot of Souls do live under and around Paektu - a lot like your Annwn, eh? I have been wanting to go there for some time, but now I have three more reasons to go, don't I?" she said, staring into Willy's eyes. They all broke out smiling.

"You will always be welcome, Mei", he said over his embarrassment.

"Well, one day - you can all count on it. However, back to the problem before us. Do you see that encampment down there and to the left? They call it Pyeonghwama-eul, Pyeonghwamacul, or Pyeonghwa village - 화마을 in Korean, for it is in the most northern part of north Korea. It is registered as a mining village, but that is just to hide its true raison d'être. It is a slaughterhouse for animals useful to traditional East Asian 'medicines', and the Amur is its speciality. Our sources tell us that they have three Amurs in there now and that they are going to kill two tonight. The other one has been spared for now because she is pregnant, but she only has a few weeks to go. Perhaps they will let her wean her cub, but then… well, you know.

"Anyway, our surface-dwelling friends tell us that two will definitely be dispatched tonight, and that they plan to release all three back into the wild".

"What is the plan?" asked Becky

"It blows a rain or a snow storm here really often, and we are informed that there will almost definitely be one tonight. Our Surface friends will release the cats under cover of that storm, and our job is to make sure that they don't kill the cats before the storm arrives".

"By spooking the poachers?" asked Sarah.

"Exactly!"

"Great!" she replied, "What fun! I'm looking forward to this. I presume that you have contacts in the camp".

"Certainly. The camp cook and her husband are psychic and with us. Their names are Li Wei and Wang Jing. Jing is the only woman in the camp, and Wei is tall and will be wearing a Chelsea football shirt. Can you see the wind picking up?"

"Perhaps", said Willy, "but it was blowing a hoolie before, compared to what I, we, are used to. We used to think that our mountain was windy, but this is something else!"

"We live on a hill, Willy, we only call it a mountain. This is a real one".

"I suppose so… it's what you're used to, isn't it?"

"Look! Movement in the bushes below the camp. They are bringing the generator back from the repair shop. Jing sabotaged the equipment they normally use to kill the tigers. I mean, it wouldn't have stopped them really, but it is easier to use a generator to deliver a fatal shock, than heating a poker to red-hot and , er, inserting it from behind, which is the traditional method of dispatching the poor creatures".

"Oh, my God! Can people stoop so low? That is barbaric! No, what is a word for ten times worse than barbaric? It's sadistic, it's sick!"

"People have done as bad, and even worse to each other – Vlad the Impaler - and even animals, Willy? Remember badger baiting? Bear baiting was before our last life, but the same thing…"

"Yes, OK. So, what is happening now, Mei?"

"It depends on them really. Perhaps, they'll eat first, or perhaps, they'll get on with the job. I know that I wouldn't be able to eat afterwards though, so we may have thirty or forty minutes… We need the storm to arrive within half an hour".

"What do you reckon?" asked Becky.

"It could do… it could do. The weather changes very quickly around our mountain, but it is unpredictable too".

"What if it doesn't though?"

"Well, in that case, we will have to delay them!"

"Do you have something in mind?" asked Sarah.

"Oh, most definitely, my friend, we scare the bejeebers out of them!"

"I like the sound of that!" replied Sarah enthusiastically.

"It is quite easy to do, and they deserve it. The people surrounding this mountain have believed for hundreds, if not thousands, of years that their ancestral and Spiritual home is inside or underneath this mountain… Rather like your Annwn, yes?"

"You will always be welcome in Annwn, Mei", said Willy. The others nodded their agreement.

"Thank you. So, like I was saying, they believe that the place is 'haunted', so to speak, and we can play into that belief to disrupt their plans. It has worked many times before, but it has only a temporary effect. Sooner or later, people always come back… not always the same people, and not always to the same place, but the trade goes on, and on, and on. It is against the law, of course, but bribery and corruption are rife among poorly-paid officials, and an Amur is worth several years' salary… for soldiers too.

"Look! There's Jing!" Mei stood up and waved enthusiastically. Jing nodded back, and banged two sticks together, a sign that dinner was ready, and then went back inside her hut. Five men appeared from various places and sat at a table outside Jing's hut. "That should give us at least twenty minutes, but we still need a storm".

"So, if this trade in tiger parts is illegal, how do they go about distribution? Bribery and corruption, OK, I get all that, but officials still have to be seen to be doing their jobs, surely?" asked Willy.

"Yes… they do… but," Mei was trying to follow the men's conversation over dinner, but did not want to appear rude to Willy. "But, er, it is not so difficult to achieve. They are definitely going to electrocute the two male cats this evening. They want to get rid of the cats and spend some time in a city having 'a great time in the bars' on the proceeds. Er, the jungle around here is dense, so it is easy to transport animal parts in rucksacks. There are also many streams to float small boats down, and there are two roads to Samjiyon aeroport. They are discussing the weather… they think that the storm may hold off… No, wait two for and three against a storm. Yes, the aeroport is about fifty-five kilometres from here… about an hour's drive. If they get the contraband that far, well, private aircraft can disperse it anywhere within hundreds of kilometres! It would be almost impossible to trace - like finding a needle in a haystack, eh?"

Mei was smiling, but her friends were not, suddenly saddened by the very thought, greys and blues swirling through their Auras. "We had better not let them get away with it, storm or no storm!" said Becky defiantly. She looked up at the Heavens, and although the wind was blowing, there didn't seem to be any rain or snow in the air.

Suddenly, there was a movement down below. The men were getting up from the table. "That was lovely, Jing, my dear. Fantastic, but we'd better be getting on with it now", said someone who they guessed might be the boss.

"Aw! Let's have a couple more drinks before we do that", said Wei.

"He's stalling for time", said Mei, "Good man, keep it up!".

"It's such a grizzly job. I need to be two sheets to the wind before I can face killing such beautiful creatures as those, Zhang Jie", complained Wei to Zhang Jie, the man who had spoken before - the camp boss.

"None of us likes doing it, but it pays the bills and keeps Mr Big sweet… OK, one more beer and a couple of shots of Soju, but then we have to do it. You've got twenty minutes, and not a second longer". They all sat down again relieved at the reprieve. Wei reached over, took five bottles of Taedonggang beer from the crate beside him and handed them around. Half a large bottle of 53% Soju was already on the table.

"So, there you have it", explained Mei, "We have twenty minutes to pray for a storm, or organise an alternative. That's what that man in the green camouflage gear just said. He's the boss here. Come on, I'll show you the tigers. Follow me into that cave over there". They drifted down to the level of the men at the table but about fifty metres behind them and entered the cave. it was pitch-black inside because the generator hadn't been connected up yet, but it stood there ready for use - a large 15,000 Watt generator. The darkness was not a problem for the four friends, but the camp had been using kerosene lamps while the generator had been out of action. Nobody liked the noise that it made anyway, so it was only fired up when needed.

"Here are our beautiful Amurs. I love that word", she chuckled, "it makes me think of the French word for love 'amour', and I do love these big cats so". It occurred to Sarah not for the first time that night, that Mei was a linguist. Spirit beings spoke by thought transference, telepathy, and that comes in a kind of universal language, but it still has to be learned, although most found it easier than learning spoken languages.

Mei indicated three cages which were each just big enough to hold a three-metre Amur tiger. There was no room for exercise. One of the cats growled in a low rumble, but not fiercely when it spotted the friends, and that alerted the other two, which might have been sleeping. They were used to being comforted by Spirit helpers, although there was no-one there at that moment. Willy stepped forward, put his hand through the bars and stroked the cat's head. It purred like a kitten but more loudly. "There's a good boy! You like that, don't you? Of course you do… a bit of love and attention? Who wouldn't? We'll soon have you and your pals out of here, and once you get out of this cave, run like the wind and never come back again. You hear?"

"Look, this is how they do it", said Mei. "The cages are winched up, one at a time, moved outside with that frame and lowered into a hollow they have dug in the ground which is full of water. Then they attach jump leads from the generator to the bars of the cage and zap! One dead tiger! At least, that's the theory. Despite all that, just as with 'Old Sparky' in Sing Sing Correctional Facility in New York, it doesn't always work out according to plan. It can take minutes… minutes of agony for the tiger. Most of the men don't like to watch either, but someone has to".

Sarah had found the pregnant tiger, and was soothing her. Suddenly, another image appeared, and it startled the three friends from Wales. A huge Siberian tiger was walking through the entrance of the cave. They were not afraid, because it couldn't harm them. It was also already dead. However, its size was so impressive. It looked around the cave, then walked over to Sarah, cuddled up to the female tiger and licked her face. Mei could not help smiling at her friends' facial expressions. "Let me introduce you to Gāng zhǎo - Steel Claws - or that's what we call him anyway. He often visits the female. Perhaps, he's her husband. He almost certainly was killed here and not long ago, because, as you know, animals don't usually remain in visible Spirit form unless they have a strong emotional bond with someone or something. We think that he was murdered within the last couple of weeks. Perhaps they were captured together, or perhaps they didn't have a physical relationship, but know each other from here. I doubt that we will ever know for certain.

"It is time to prepare. The men will be coming for the first cage in a few minutes. Try to relax the cats, they will be frightened when the commotion starts. I'm going to have a word with Jing while she's doing the washing up. Oh, where is that storm when you need it?" Becky moved to the third cat and began to talk to it as if it were a kitten.

Two men entered the cave and wheeled the generator outside. They struggled to get the small wheels of the carriage to cross the uneven floor of the cave and the rocks outside. They could not use it inside because of carbon monoxide poisoning, but they were not taking it far. A few minutes later, they returned for the first tiger. The three friends were horrified as they manoeuvred the A-frame and winch into position above the tiger's cage. The cat didn't have much room, but it tried to launch an attack on the men, who recoiled from the ferocity of its snarling. Gāng zhǎo stood up to defend his lady, but was as powerless as the human Spirits were, since they were unable to move anything physically.

When they had recovered from the initial shock of the tiger's reaction, they returned to the cage, winched it 150mm up from the ground, and began to push it outside. The three friends were wondering where Mei was, and whether they should do anything to help the distressed animal.

"It is tough", said Sarah, "but this is not our show, so just sit tight and be ready. It doesn't seem that any of the bad guys can see us, so there's no need to conceal ourselves. I know what you are going through, but there really is nothing that we can do".

They watched as the cage was wheeled over the water pit and the generator started up. Sarah was trying to get through to Mei, but was having no luck. As the generator spluttered into life, hundreds of shining silvery orbs rushed past them from the bowls of the mountain at the back of the cave.

The poachers had seen the orbs before, but never in such numbers. They streamed out of the cave and around the camp like dead leaves in a furious dust devil. Jing and Wei started screaming that the Ancestors were angry in an attempt to create fear and panic. The three Welsh friends joined the thong and harassed the men as much as possible.

And then the rain came in torrents and the men were slipping and sliding about in disarray. Wei "accidentally" ran into the jump leads, disconnecting them from the generator and "fell" onto the cage, where he was able to draw back the bolt that locked the cage. He was putting himself at great danger from the frightened cat, but a host of Spirit beings were trying to placate the tiger and urged it to make its escape. It bounded out of the cage, and fell in the mud because it had cramp from being locked up for so long. Seconds later, fear overcame pain and it disappeared into the jungle.

Meanwhile, Jing had slipped into the cave and unbolted the remaining cages. She too was taking a big risk, but the men had already fled their nightmarish camp, and Jing had confidence that the animals would run rather than attack her, as she had been feeding them since their arrival.

She was right too, encouraged by Spirit to run, they paid Jing no attention. Gāng zhǎo followed his mate, and Willy followed them both deep into the jungle. They ran and ran through the belting, rain and wind through thick undergrowth, densely-packed trees and bushes leaping over dead logs and boulders as if the very Devil were behind them. After about a kilometre, the she became tired and lolled, panting on a rock, elevated out of the sodden soil. Her friend was ever beside her and Willy was too, although he kept a respectable distance of a few metres to give them their own space. He could see that the pregnant she was worn out. She had been fed earlier, and there was no shortage of water. She just needed rest.

Willy stayed with the cats, but explained to Sarah what he was doing. He just wanted to see that the she was safe, and perhaps also learn something more about the tigers that he had come to love so much. It was a rare opportunity for a man, albeit a Spirit, from Wales to be able to study the interaction of a live Siberian tiger in her own environment, but also with a tiger Spirit Guide accompanying her. He had never heard of such a study, and was sure that a chance such as this would not come around again. Sarah agreed, and even asked to join him to take a look for herself from time to time.

This meant putting their own project on hold for a while, as far as Willy was concerned, but his two friends could continue making arrangements, which he would comply with without hesitation.

Over time, Willy wasn't sure how long, but then he never had been interested in hours or days, he became friends with the two tigers, and even witnessed the birth of their three cubs. He became especially friendly with Gāng zhǎo, and when Willy returned to Annwn and his 'normal life' after ten weeks, the big cat would often visit him unexpectedly.

7. The Patel's

"Aren't the twins gorgeous, Sanjay?" asked their mother of her husband, as they stared through the glass wall of the neonatal intensive care unit.

"Yes, my dear. They are beautiful. Don't worry about them. They are in good hands. The Heath Hospital is the best in the land, and if you are ever not happy with the treatment they are receiving, we will move them to wherever you want". He put a comforting right arm around his wife, and gave her shoulder a squeeze as a tear escaped from his left eye. He hoped that his wife wouldn't see it in his reflection. He had no reason for concern though, since his wife, Carol, was struggling with her own emotions and teary eyes.

"They look so helpless, and vulnerable…" she muttered as Sanjay tightened his grip on her. "I just can't bear it! I want to hold, and hug them, and make everything all right for them… the poor little mites…" They were looking at their two-week-old children - a boy and a girl - who were suffering from some unknown problem, which the doctors had not yet been able to identify. They were lying in a double cot, and were still and silent except for an occasional movement of their heads.

"I'm certain that they can feel the love flowing from us to them and from them to each other", comforted Sanjay, and meant it too.

"I so want to believe that, Sanjay, my love… I really do"

"Didn't the doctor say that there was nothing to worry about?"

"Well, not really. The doctor said that the odds were in their favour… that's not quite the same. Please don't patronise me. I know you mean well, but… you know…"

"Yes, sorry. I said it to cheer myself up as much as you". She patted the hand that was still around her shoulder. "Sorry, my dear, I know.

There are five other babies in the NICU… two more than yesterday. Someone else must have given birth to twins very recently. Those two are in a double cot just like ours".

"I envy you", whispered Sanjay. "Tomorrow you will be able to begin that Kangaroo Mother Care, won't you? I wonder if they would allow KMC for fathers… KFC. No, they won't allow babies to have KFC, will they? They don't even have any teeth yet!" They both chuckled, and Carol gave her husband a light thump on the chest.

"You are daft sometimes, but I love you".

"I love you too. Still, it would be nice to help with the skin contact, although I perfectly understand that the staff want to keep the risk of cross-infection as low as possible. Come on, you look dead beat. Let's get a take-away and go home. There's nothing we can do here, and you have a big day tomorrow. You will need to be strong so that your vitality can flow to the children".

∞

The following day Sanjay accompanied his wife to the hospital, and waited for her to be prepared to be admitted to the NICU and take her place in one of the full-size beds in order to receive their children. When she was in place, Sanjay received notification that he could go down to the viewing pane as before. He walked as quickly as possible, while remaining safe and dignified, to the NICU. He could scarcely hold back the tears when he saw Carol holding their little boy and girl. She was beaming from ear to ear, but couldn't wave back because she held an infant in the crook of each arm. He was vaguely aware of another man also peering in through the viewing pane, but had already spotted a woman in a bed near his wife, who was also holding two babies in her arms. He looked at the man, who was several metres away, smiled and raised his thumb, but the stranger just appeared to sniff, and look back at the other woman, who Sanjay presumed was his wife. After ten minutes, the curtains were drawn around the ladies' beds so that they could undo their gowns to allow full contact with their babies.

Sanjay said "Well, the show's over for now. That's my wife and twins in there. Are the other two yours? Beautiful babies, and mother. My name's Sanjay by the way. We've got a lot in common!" He advanced towards the stranger arm outstretched. The man barely looked at him, said something under his breath and left the room defiantly.

Sanjay was loath to follow on his heels. *Did I really hear that correctly? Did he really say 'Bloody foreigners', or am I being paranoid?*

Sanjay had been born in Splott, Cardiff thirty years before to Indian immigrants who had borrowed enough from some members of their families to establish a corner shop in the busy street market area. Footfall was high, and his parents had been good business people. They had also worked long hours to repay the loan, and expand their business. They had retired from actual physical work now, but still enjoyed hanging around the shops, much to the annoyance of their managers and staff, because Mr. Patel, especially, could not resist 'giving them the benefit of his experience', which they referred to as meddling. If he had had his way, he would not have retired, but ill-health had forced his hand. He could no longer stand on his feet for protracted periods of time. Sanjay's mother, on the other hand, was less reluctant to retire because she still had her beloved kitchen, and was looking forward to grandchildren. Sanjay's would be her first, and in her opinion, he had already waited too long to provide them.

They had all experienced racism. His parents more than Sanjay, because society had been less tolerant in the Sixties when they had arrived. Nevertheless, it still raised its ugly head from time to time, and Sanjay had learned to live with the gut-twisting ache of knowing that someone didn't like him, despite never having met him. It was mentally disturbing too, because any thinking person had to ponder the question 'why?', even if they had gone over the subject many, many times in their minds before. Racism was irrational, but that didn't mean that it was easily dismissed.

Life as a young boy in Splott had been tough, but he had done well at school and had moved away to study economics and business studies at the London School of Economics. After university, where he received a first with honours, he had returned to be near his parents, and become active in the Splott branch of the Labour Party. He had become a local activist three years before, and was deemed a high-flyer. It was at a branch meeting that he had met Carol. They were married within a year after a whirlwind romance.

Carol had studied law at Cardiff University, and had graduated two years before. It had been mutual love at first sight. She was of white Welsh parents, whose families had lived in Cardiff for generations, although they had originally come from Anglesey in the mid-Nineteenth Century to work on the building of the docks in Barry and Cardiff. Her father was a structural engineer, and her mother was a relief teacher. Carol had yet to find full-time employment, but was happy to work part-time especially now that they had the twins, who might possibly be suffering complications.

Carol had suffered a form of discrimination too from time to time, but she had tried to keep it from her husband. It usually went along the lines of "can't find a White guy who wants you, eh?" It hurt just as much as what Sanjay had to put up with, but she tried to console herself by reaffirming to herself that the people who taunted her were morons. When it had happened when she was with Sanjay, she had had problems restraining him.

None of that made any difference now. She and her husband were happy, and she was confident that their children would be too… soon, if the babies realised what danger they were in, which she doubted.

Sanjay was more sanguine. He was a strong Buddhist, and firmly believed that their children would survive, although it was only a feeling - he could not explain why he thought it. He knew that Carol shared his beliefs, although she had come to them, whereas Sanjay had been born into Buddhism. He believed in Karma as an Immutable Law, and he had a strong, good feeling about their children, but he hoped that they would not have to undergo the problems of racism that previous generations of children of immigrant parents had experienced.

They had encountered mild resistance to their relationship from both sets of in-laws at first too. Sanjay's parents were used to him dating girls of all sorts of ethnic backgrounds, but they had secretly hoped that he would eventually settle down with a 'nice Indian girl' from a respectable family. Carol's parents had known her views on racism for a decade or more, but had never contemplated the possibility that she would not marry a white Brit. None of the in-laws caused much of a fuss though, and everybody got on very well when they had family gatherings, which were on the major Buddhist and Christian religious festivals and the occasional birthday. Their mutual grandchildren would bring them all even closer together in a natural way.

Naming the children was a potential source of conflict, but the parents had given it a lot of thought. They hadn't actually decided on any names yet, but they were tending towards giving one an Indian first name, and a Welsh middle name, and the other a Welsh first name and an Indian middle name. Who was to get which combination was still also undecided, but it occupied much of the thought of the six people with an interest. Carol's father, Dylan, ever the practical one, had said that he thought that an Indian name on a job application might prejudice the selection team against that person, but when Carol had pointed out that they were not going to be changing their surname from Patel any time soon, he gave up.

∞

Sitting at home one afternoon, Carol said, "Mary told me today that you had spoken to her husband. You hadn't said anything…"

"Mary? Mary who?"

"The mother of the other twins in the NICU. You know".

"Oh, that Mary… I didn't actually meet him, and I've never spoken to his wife Mary either for that matter".

"Mary said that you had spoken to him. His name is Jonathan, and he doesn't like to be called John. He can be a little difficult sometimes, she said… Mary, that is".

"Can he? The other day, I assumed that it was his wife in the bed next to yours, and I said 'Hello' or something like that… and I gave him the thumbs-up sign. That's all. It wasn't a conversation. He didn't even reply. He just walked off. Perhaps, he didn't hear me… It doesn't matter".

"Mary said that her Jonathan can be a bit difficult because he doesn't like Paki's and immigrants. Maybe he did hear you. Are you sure that he didn't say anything? Sanjay? Come on! Out with it! I always know when you're trying to hide something from me. What is it, darling?"

"It's nothing really. Let's just let it drop, shall we?" *Why am I behaving like this? I've done nothing wrong. Why not just tell her that her friend's husband is a shit-head, idiot racist?* "All right, I think he did say something, but I'm not absolutely sure. Perhaps he said, 'Bloody immigrants'… perhaps".

"He did say that, didn't he, Sanjay? Be honest with me. I know that these things still hurt, but they aren't your fault".

"For Christ's sake! Aren't there enough brown and black people over here, and haven't we been here long enough to be given the benefit of the doubt yet? Indians have been here for a hundred years already, and I ain't a Paki! I'm Welsh, and my parents are naturalised Indians, who have been working… no, slogging their guts out for nearly fifty years! Most white people can't say that! Well, probably not, anyway. Sometimes, I wonder why my parents came to this bloody country!"

"OK, Sanjay, OK. I am on your side, and you know that your parents came here to make a better life…"

"But is it better? Really? More money, yes, but a better life? I'm not so sure. I've been back to the old country, and I liked it…"

"No, you didn't. You said that the village was dreadful, and smelly, I think you said. You only liked to have more money than the rest of your family there…"

"Oh, that's not true! Frankly, that was embarrassing, but it was nice to be able to help".

"OK, Sanjay! OK! Enough is enough! This always happens when you are upset. We are on the same side. We are not the problem, and you will probably never see Mr. Jonathan Bloody Racist again because our children can come home tomorrow!"

"Really, darling? That's wonderful news! You have made my day, my week, my life even! Er, but what are we going to call our little Janet and John? We can't welcome them into their new home as he and she".

"No, we cannot, but during the hours that they have been lying with me, I thought that it would be nice to give them the same name but in Welsh and Hindi. What do you think?"

"Yes, that sounds great. That should keep everyone happy".

∞

"OK, Sanjay, are you ready? On three. One, two, three!"

In order to preserve their sanity and peace between their parents, Sanjay and Carol both phoned their mothers at exactly the same time with exactly the same news… no more and no less.

"Hello, Mum. How are you and Dad? Great! Yes, we're fine too, and so are the twins. They're what I'm phoning about actually. Two bits of news: one: we can bring them home tomorrow… Yes, fantastic, isn't it? And two: we have decided on what to call them. The boy will be Emrys Amar Patel, which means ' immortal' in Welsh and Hindi, as you surely know already, and the girl will be Alesha Seren Patel, which means 'star' in both languages. So, together, they are the immortal, or eternal star. What do you think? Are you happy with that?"

Both sets of grandparents were completely satisfied. It made the new parents sigh with relief.

"I suppose we should start looking around for schools for them now", said Sanjay, so Carol hit him with a pillow.

"There's plenty of time for that, but you are right. It is something that we will have to consider soon. I mean Splott has good schools… you did all right here, but do we want something better? Do you want a private school, or just a state school, but in a better area? Because if you want the state option, we are going to have to move… buy a house even. That won't be cheap, and we have less than five years to save up". The reality of parenthood was beginning to dawn on them, but they were both geared up for it and relished the challenge.

When they brought the children back to their rented apartment a couple of streets away from the Patel's shop, the spare room had been redecorated as a nursery in primary colours and hundreds of pounds worth of toys and furniture lay thoughtfully placed around the room. It was clear that little Emrys and Alesha would want for nothing - at least in the early years of their lives.

∞

Carol attended a postnatal clinic with the twins two weeks after they had come home on the advice of the health visitor, and was pleasantly surprised to see someone there that she already knew. "Mary! I'm so glad to see you here. I wasn't looking forward to being with a bunch of strangers all talking about how bright the little kids were. How are the twins? Oh, aren't they gorgeous? Two beautiful little girls, and they're identical too. You must be so proud of them".

"Yes, I am. So, is Jonathan. Yes, I was a bit nervous about coming here too. Some mothers, and fathers, do get carried away with it all don't they? Especially first-time parents. Oh, sorry, Emrys and Alesha are your first, aren't they? These are our first too. Shall we go for a cup of tea and a cake after we're done here? We can have a natter and compare notes. What do you think? Go on, say you will".

"Oh, yes, of course! I'd like that. Yes, they are our first too. It is very difficult trying to remember that not everyone is as fascinated by their antics as we are, isn't it?".

"They don't know what they're missing, or they've forgotten how exciting it is to watch tiny human beings learn how to control their bodies, and… er, well interact with their surroundings and fellow beings, I suppose".

"I had no idea how much I'd enjoy being a mother before we had the twins. I've enjoyed every minute of it – even the birth, which was not easy to say the least!"

It was the start of a deep friendship. The four children got on very well together too. They would meet in the local parks, tea shops, and even at each others' houses during the day, for Mary and her family lived in Adamsdown which was an adjoining housing estate only fifteen minutes walk, or five minutes by bus or car.

It was only the husbands that kept finding excuses not to meet up, so the two families never quite fully integrated. This was not for lack of encouragement on behalf of the wives, but the two men kept finding excuses, so they eventually gave up.

Leaving Annwn

8. Entente Cordiale

"Oh, Carol! I can't wake Ceridwen! I think she's… she's dead! What can I do?" Mary was crying on the phone. She was obviously in the grip of a fierce panic.

"Calm down a little, Mary. Have you phoned an ambulance yet?"

"No, I haven't phoned anyone yet… only you! Quickly, tell me what to do! I couldn't bear it if she died… What will we do without her? Oh, my God, and how would I tell Jonathan? He'll blame me. Help me, for Christ's Sake, Mary! Help me and little Ceridwen!"

"OK, take deep breaths. I'll phone an ambulance, and I'll be on my way in two minutes. I'll have to bring the twins because Sanjay's at work… Jonathan is working away too, isn't he?"

"Yes, he's in Oxford, or some bloody place! Please hurry!"

It was just after ten o'clock in the morning, and Carol was thankful that she was already dressed and had fed the twins, who were taking a nap. She bundled them into their carry cot, strapped that into the back seat of her car and headed for Mary's.

"Oh, thank God you're here. I'm pretty sure that she's dead, or in a coma. Please let it be in a coma. There's the ambulance outside! Would you let them in, please?"

Ceridwen was pronounced dead fifteen minutes later at the hospital. The cause of death was unknown. The inquest attributed her passing to Sudden Infant Death Syndrome.

∞

"Thank you for coming to little Ceridwen's funeral", said Jonathan to Carol and Sanjay after the service and interment. "You were a great comfort to Mary, Carol, I don't know what she would have done without you. We decided not to hold a formal repast, or reception. It didn't seem appropriate somehow for someone so young, but I don't think that we could have handled it anyway. Still, we're going to go home and have a few drinks, just Mary and me, and her mother - she's inconsolable. It'll be a pretty miserable affair, but you are both welcome to join us, if you've got no other plans".

Sanjay didn't want to go because of Jonathan, but he knew how difficult the last week had been for Mary and her family, so said nothing. He was willing to abide by his wife's decision. He looked at her and blinked slowly. "Yes, Jonathan. Thank you. We'd love to come and pay our respects, wouldn't we, Sanjay?"

"Yes, of course. Thank you for the invite, Jonathan". He held out his hand, and this time Jonathan took it and shook it warmly. "We'll follow you in the car".

Back in their house, Mary and her mother laid on a spread of sandwiches, pastries and cakes, which looked enough to feed ten times their number. There was wine, beer and spirits aplenty too, which Jonathan and his mother soon attacked with gusto. "What can I get you, Sanjay? Tea, or coffee? You don't drink alcohol, I suppose?"

Here we go again! He's stereotyped me as a teetotal Muslim or Buddhist. I'll show the conceited bastard! "I'll have whatever you're having".

"Oh, a renegade, are you? I didn't think that your sort drank alcohol. White man's medicine, eh?" he laughed out loud. "OK! Two pints of Brains bitter and two double Jameson's coming right up!"

What a prick! "We are not all teetotal, the same as not all Christians are devout, and as for White man's medicine, the word 'alcohol' is Arabic, and Arabs are closer to my colour than yours, so you white people probably stole the invention from them, like you stole resources from all of your colonies!"

"Hey, boys, boys, boys! Stop all this bickering, will you? Remember what day it is! It's poor little Ceridwen's funeral. Please act accordingly!", said Mary's mother, Gwladys. Mary and Carol applauded, "Hear, hear!"

"Yes, I apologise for my bad behaviour", said Sanjay.

"So, do I", agreed Jonathan. "Truce for today, for little Ceridwen's sake. Deal?"

"Deal!" repeated Sanjay, and they clinked glasses.

"Let's sit at the table in the bay window. Mary can't drink, because she's still breast-feeding. Carol's the same, I suppose, so that just leaves me, you and Mum, don't it, Mum? And I think you'd rather be with the kids than with me. That just leaves me and my new mate, Sanjay". They carried their drinks to the table, which had some of the food laid out on it and sat down. "Help yourself to sarnies, Sanjay. You'll have to look out for the ham sandwiches. Any of these got ham in 'em, Mary. Sanjay's got to watch out for them?"

"The ones on the blue plate are ham, Sanjay".

"It doesn't matter, Mary. I eat ham and pork. I'm a Buddhist, not a Muslim". *The ignorance of some people is quite astounding. I don't know how long I can sit here with this idiot.* "So, Jonathan, Carol tells me you're a travelling salesman. What do you sell?"

"Office supplies. It covers a wide range these days. You know, computers, printers and the like besides paper and Biros. In fact, there's not much call for Biros any more".

"I run an office for my parents' shop, but am looking to branch out. Maybe I could put some business your way".

"No, I don't think so. Your shop is out of my patch. It'd be poaching, and that is frowned upon. Thanks all the same. I could tip the local rep the wink to contact you though. Sam, she deals with Wales and the West. Good looker too, is Sam", and he winked at Sanjay. "Ready for another? Another round coming up!"

"So, you're a Buddhist, are you, Sanjay. That's very interesting. Carol is too, Mum… and she was before she met Sanjay, weren't you, Carol?"

"Yes. It makes more sense to me personally than our state religions". The two new mothers sat on the floor with the three children, the two fathers sat near the window, and Mary's mother sat on the couch between the two groups, dragging one or the other group into mutual conversations from time to time.

"Me, I don't believe in no God any more" said Gwladys. "How can there be one with all the wars in the world and all the little kiddies suffering... and what sort of God would snatch our poor little Ceridwen away so early in her life? There is no God, and no justice!" Tears ran down her cheeks.

"There, there, Mum. Don't take on so. What's done is done, and Ceridwen is in Heaven now. She won't suffer any more".

"Suffer? She never suffered at all in the first place. She had a lovely home, and all the love that any parents and a grandmother could give her. She even had a lovely little sister. She never suffered, so why did your God have to take her away from it all - us all?"

"What do your lot reckon on the subject, Sanjay? You Buddhists…" His head was beginning to sway a little from the drink.

"Oh, you don't want to get into all that now", interjected Carol. "That's a subject for another day".

"I disagree", said Jonathan. "Today is the perfect day for such a discussion, all things considered… our baby girl considered. Don't you agree, Mary?" Mary didn't like to disagree with her husband in public, so nodded, but said nothing. "There you are. Mary wants to know what Buddhists think; I want to know what Buddhists think; and our dear old Mum finds it interesting, so the floor is all yours, Sanjay".

"All right. If you insist". Carol caught his eye and pleaded for restraint with her facial expression. "There is not only one Buddhist belief. Just as there is not just one Christian belief, or one Islamic belief. However, most of us, Buddhists, that is, believe in a God, but it could be called nature. God does not go around snatching babies from healthy lives or allowing wars. Every Soul is the master of its own destiny, and bears full responsibility for all of its actions. We see life as a lesson, a course at school, if you like… or university. You sign up for a course, and then learn your lessons during your life. Some Souls choose an easy course, and others a more difficult one. This accounts for much of the diversity in life".

"OK, so why do babies die young?" asked Gwladys.

"To stick with the analogy of school courses; a course is expensive and it has to be seen through to the end. Say that my course is seventy-five years long, but I commit suicide at seventy, then I would have to be reborn and die at five years old. It is that simple. God, as such, doesn't play a rôle in it. It is just one of the Immutable Laws of nature - one of God's Laws, if you like".

"Bollocks! What a load of cobblers!" exclaimed Jonathan.

"Not in this house, and not in front of the children..." wailed Mary, and started to cry again when she realised what she had said. Jonathan went to her, comforted her, apologised to everyone, and returned to his seat.

"OK, OK! Here's one for you... if there's a God, how can he be watching over all of us at all times?"

"He, She or It cannot. It doesn't make sense... Unless, you believe in Guardian Angels, or Spirit Guides as we call them. If everybody has a Spirit Guide then that god-like being can watch over its ward. It makes far more sense. The Christian way of looking at it has just become a little warped". He watched Jonathan bristle at the implied criticism, and saw Carol's concern. *I don't care if I upset the cocky bastard.*

"I like the idea", said Mary. "Nobody took our little Ceridwen away, or allowed her to die... it was her own decision. She was only visiting us... like a foster child. Now, she has gone back to her proper way of life. Does it mean that we will never see her again?"

"That is really up to you and her. No-one can make her visit you, but you did her a great favour by allowing her into your family for such a short time knowing what grief it would ultimately cause you. You helped her complete her destiny, despite the hardship that it would cause you. She will be feeling grateful. It is not at all unusual for such bonds to turn into long-lasting friendships, if you remain open to seeing her, and she wants to visit you, you may see her in your dreams, and maybe even standing before you as I am sitting before you now. Don't expect to see her as a small baby though. She may come back as a young girl... but if she wants you to, and your mind is receptive, you may have contact. I have heard of many, many such cases".

"I would like that. Yes, that would be really nice. Thank you, Sanjay. Just the thought that I may see our Ceridwen, our 'Blessed Lady' – that's what her name means – see her again one day makes me feel so much better. It's a bit like when a friend moves away. You always hope that you will meet up again one day… old school friends and the like. Don't you think so, Jonathan?"

"Yes, my dear. It is a very comforting thought, but I am still a Christian through and through and always will be!"

"The beliefs are not incompatible", said Carol. "No-one is trying to force you to change your beliefs. Sanjay is only suggesting that you keep an open mind, and see what comes to you, aren't you, Sanjay?"

"He did insist on knowing what us lot believe, but yes, an open mind is the key… or if your mind is open, no-one needs a key to get in, I suppose". He gave himself an imaginary pat on the back for thinking of that way of putting it. "When the pupil is ready, the teacher will appear'. Same sort of idea. I remember that from Religious Instruction at school".

"Where did you go to school?"

"Just locally. I was born near Splott market".

"I was born in this house".

"We were probably in rival gangs as kids".

"Yeah, probably".

"We might even have had some mutual friends".

"Nah, we didn't like the Splott Snots".

"You're probably right. We didn't like the Addams Family freaks either".

"We always hammered you at football!"

"A pussy's game! We always won at rugby. What about cricket?"

They both made disparaging noises about cricket at the same time.

The three women smiled to each other, and shook their heads, as they listened to the men reminisce and get drunk.

∞

"Hangover?" asked Carol in the kitchen the next morning.

"No! Or course not. We didn't have that much to drink".

"So, you still intend taking the three children to watch the rugby on Sunday, do you?"

"Er, yes, if everyone still wants to go by then. Er, which rugby match was that, love? It seems to have slipped my mind".

"Drunk! I knew you were drunk! You and Jonathan were planning on taking the three children to watch their first rugby match on Sunday".

"Are we all going?"

"No. Mary, Gwladys and I are going shopping, and will cook lunch, while you five go to watch the game on the local playing fields. Get them started in the right traditions early - you said. Rugby and football whenever it was convenient - said Jonathan. You are both determined to be 'hands-on Dads - you both said".

"Yes. Well, it is important, isn't it? Tradition, roots and all that… Can you pour me a cup of black coffee, please? And two paracetamols…"

"Yes, we all agree with you, but children of fourteen weeks can't see far enough to watch a game of rugby! They don't even recognise colour well enough to distinguish teams. It'll be another nine months at least before they'll be able to see the game, and probably another year or two before they can follow one, although they probably won't have the attention span to want to".

"Still, they can soak up the atmosphere, can't they, love, and start learning the words to the Welsh rugby songs early?"

"You'll be wanting a train set next", she smiled.

"It's funny that you should mention that, but I was thinking about looking at the Tri-ang Hornby range. What do you think?" Carol put his coffee and headache tablets before him and left the room laughing.

Leaving Annwn

∞

The three children grew up as triplets, and the two families grew ever closer entwined because of it. The powerhouse of the friendship was the wives, but it was blindingly obvious to everyone that the children were very, very close. As close as any children in one family could be, and far more than one would expect from unrelated kids. The parents encouraged their friendship, and one day, when Carol intimated that they were saving to move to Roath in order to get their children into a better school, Mary said that she had been thinking along the same lines.

Two years later, the Patel's and the Williams' families moved into adjacent properties overlooking Roath boating lake. The children were three years old, but were already showing remarkable communication skills for their age. All three of them even displayed a telepathic ability normally associated only with twins of the same family. Somehow, the parents realised, Enaid had managed to tap into the mental communication between Alesha and Emrys. The phenomenon baffled the local doctors, so they referred their case to educational psychologists at the Heath, who in turn suggested that they contact Potential Plus UK, which is part of the National Association for Gifted Children.

"Isn't this exciting?" squeaked Mary one afternoon as the four parents huddled around her computer and typed "Potential Plus UK" into a search engine. She clicked on the website at the top of the search results. They were all delighted to read what popped up:

> 'Potential Plus UK is often contacted by parents wanting to understand their child's learning profile in order to be able to support their educational, social and emotional needs. We believe in supporting the social, emotional and learning needs of children with high learning potential, therefore, to empower parents to support their children, we offer several assessments that offer recommendations based on their child's unique profile. Our current face-to-face assessment

centres are based in Milton Keynes and Gloucestershire'.

"Look! It says click to 'Become a member'. That's exactly what we are looking for - go on, click it, Mary", urged her husband. Mary willingly did as she was bid, in fact, she hadn't needed telling. I'm ready to join right now. How about the rest of you?"

"I think we ought to read the whole site first, and check to see if there are any alternatives", said Carol with her solicitor's hat on. It might be better if we go home now, and investigate from our own computer, while you do the same here. We can meet up tomorrow evening, and compare notes".

"Are you going off the idea, Carol?" asked Jonathan.

"No, it's not that, but this website seems to be concentrating on academic abilities. Now, I know that our kids are very bright. They are well advanced in motor skills, talking, reading et cetera, but I have a feeling that they also have psychic abilities, and I haven't seen a reference to that on this website yet. It could be there, but I want to see it and read it first".

"Yes, I think you're right, love", said Sanjay. "We don't have to rush into this right now. Tomorrow is soon enough". The Williams' looked deflated.

"Yes, all right", replied Jonathan. "Well, keep notes, and message anything interesting you find over to us and we'll do the same". Carol and Sanjay were not trying to be discouraging. They couldn't wait to begin their own investigation, but Carol had a hunch that the three children needed more than just extra academic stimulation, and Sanjay thought that she was right.

Leaving Annwn

9. The Teenage Years

Even before their teenage years, the trio had the reputation of being a 'little odd'… eccentric. From as young as five, when they first started school, they were always together, and would strongly resist any attempt to split them up. Emrys would frequently insist that water be put down for his tiger, Gāng Zhǎo or Steel Claws. Nobody could see his 'imaginary friend ' except the other two in the trio, who could be seen stroking 'thin air', as witnesses put it. It was not unheard of for children to have 'imaginary friends', but they were usually human.

It all added to their mystique.

By the age of nine they would often refer to themselves as the Immortal Star Soul. A year later, they were composing Limericks such as:

1]
In the realm where the Star Souls shine bright,
Eternal beings - pure light,
"We are the Immortal Star Soul",
Whispered the sage, the wise and the whole,
In cosmic dance, our essence knows Right.

2]
In the cosmos where energies are rife,
"We are the Eternal Star Life,"
Whispered the spirits in cosmic glee,
Dancing through the celestial sea,
Guiding us to realms beyond strife.

And Haiku, such as:

1]
Immortal star soul
Eternal Star Life
Amar, Alesha, Ruhi

2]
Eternal Star Life
Emrys Seren Enaid three
Showing Souls their Path

It had taken the teachers at school until they read the last one to realise that they were describing themselves. They later developed other names for their little group of three - even using their 'other names', after Enaid had adopted a Hindi Buddhist name meaning 'Soul', the same as her Welsh name. It was Ruhi, so in that frame of mind, they were: Amar Alesha Ruhi.

Most people found them charming at first, but then a little disconcerting, since they didn't behave like other modern children. They revelled in silence, and were hardly interested in television with the notable exception of animal programmes. They would sit staring at those for the duration without uttering a sound, although they would frequently look at each other and share an expression.

By this time, some friends, and teachers were referring to them as Indigo Children or Crystal Children, but the elderly Patel grandparents, Siddhartha and Tara, called them 'bodhisattvas' from an early age and were most reverential towards them.

"It is such an honour for a bodhisattva to enter your life!" Tara had said. "You do not seem to understand that… and we have three! It is unprecedented! Really! They must start going to the Buddhist Temple immediately, so that they may be helped most efficiently by people who recognise them for what they are".

"Carol, I don't blame you for not knowing what we are dealing with, but I thought that Sanjay might have guessed. Didn't you, son?" asked

Siddhartha.

"Yes, father, the thought was always in the back of my mind, but, well, one doesn't like to presume, eh? All parents think that their children are wonderful, don't they? I didn't want to make a fool of myself ".

"Well, between you and me, you have. Still, there is no time to waste now. They need extra help in their formative years... while they are children". The children had been eight years old then, and they had been attending the Temple every week ever since.

In truth, Sanjay had resisted taking them earlier, because he had wanted them to grow up free of any cultural baggage, but now he had been outvoted. Carol welcomed the idea, and went with the extended family every week. Enaid had resented not being taken that first time, and made such a fuss that not only she, but her parents as well, attended the Cardiff Buddhist Temple the following week.

The three children had taken to the experience like ducks to water, but Enaid's parents had found it tough going at first. They stuck with it though, because they could see the benefit that the monks and the community had on the children. Soon, they would realise that they too were being affected.

For the sake of balance, they also started to attend The Gateway Spiritualist Church in Northcott Street, which was also not far from their homes in Roath. The state school that they attended was Church of Wales, but the Sunday School that they sometimes went to was Catholic. They also sometimes went to Llandaff Cathedral to listen to a service and sing in the fantastically acoustic nave. Singing is a major pastime in Wales - it is not called *The Land of Song* for nothing. They enjoyed singing in school, in church, and at the various matches they attended - especially the rugby. Sanjay didn't want anyone to ever be able to say that he had bent his children's minds.

In their short lives, the power of the children had been enough to turn a racist into the family friend of Indian Buddhists, and make him interested enough in Buddhism to attend Temple services. One day, when tipsy at a football match, he had even admitted to Sanjay that he had sought the solace of a Buddhist Temple on more than one occasion when he was working away and he either felt lonely or sales were going badly.

Sanjay found such a revelation touching coming from a man who had been so rude to him because of his colour only a few years before.

∞

Everywhere the children went, strangers assumed that they were triplets. Nobody had ever fathomed why, but sometimes the children corrected them by saying that they were a trio, a triad, or even a triumvirate, and sometimes they just let it go. However, the odd thing was, that despite their slight 'strangeness', everybody took to them. Jonathan said that it was because they were so inclusive. They had a natural gift for making people feel wanted as part of the gang - not their gang, but the community that they too were part of. He said that they exuded a calmness that was missing in most people's lives and that most kids of their age usually only made it worse.

By thirteen years of age, the children were raising money for charity mostly by singing. Their favourite charities were involved with the homeless in Cardiff, and to a lesser extent in Barry, because the problem there was less acute.

Christmas was one of their favourite times of the year because it was easier to raise more money by Carol Singing. They sang with the church choirs in the street, would join in with the Salvation Army choir on Queen Street, and would also go door to door, when their parents had the time to accompany them. They consistently earned more for charity than their peer groups, but they never behaved proudly or haughtily. If anyone wanted to join them in their endeavours, they were made to feel welcome. The children's company was sought out by people of all ages, and their reputation for friendliness and an ability to succeed was becoming legendary.

Mary thought that it was only a matter of time before they would be featured in a local newspaper. Their parents were already worried about the effect that that might have on the children and upon themselves. They were mostly concerned that the press might call them 'nutty' or worse because of their references to their ghost tiger.

It was a genuine concern. People, in general, distrusted what they couldn't understand, and the children definitely fell into that category. Even their own parents hardly knew what was going on in their heads, because they seemed to keep so much to themselves. To a close observer, it was blindingly obvious that the three children were communicating with each other in a way that could not be overheard.

This, coupled with the tiger, could easily be used against them by the right-wing press. Their parents worried even more when they opened their first blog and social media pages with titles around the theme of 'Celestial Support' and 'The Star Movement'. People who had a room for rent, or something to donate were encouraged to leave online contact details, and the homeless would leave a simple wish list. The WhatsApp, Instagram, Facebook, Snapchat, and TikTok pages were an instant success. The triad devised a way of cross-posting messages to all the social media sites for maximum coverage.

Within a couple of years, the three teenagers, along with dozens of other volunteers, were organising their own special variation of the popular soup kitchens run by the traditional charities. Their idea was to seek out the housebound, old and infirm, and encourage them to cook for the homeless. Some people baked cakes, others prepared a few extra platefuls when they cooked their own daily meals. This was especially easy for parents whose children had recently left home to seek further education or work. Grandmothers loved to feel useful again, but people from all walks of life joined in. The group of helpers, called Star Assistants, would provide the volunteer cooks, or Star Chefs, with boxes to hold the food that they had cooked, then these boxes would be collected by arrangement, or delivered, and paid for from funds that had been collected. Regular contributors were given Star aprons, and customers were asked to contribute what they could afford, and given a

Star badge to wear on their lapel whatever they had donated. Customers with badges often greeted each other on the street as if they were members of a secret, privileged club.

The movement was an immediate success among the inhabitants of the working-class suburbs like Splott, Adamsdown and Tremorfa, and the Star meal boxes were handed out wherever the homeless gathered, but especially in Queen Street, around Cardiff Castle, and the city centre in general.

One day, the phone rang in the Patel household. "Good morning, am I speaking to Carol Patel?"

"You phoned me. Please identify yourself".

"Yes, of course. Please excuse my bad manners. My name is Lindsay Lauper. I'm with the Cardiff Gazette. I'd like to do an article on the three children and the Star Movement. Isn't it wonderful? When would it be convenient to talk to you, Carol?"

Carol wanted time to think, although she had been dreading this phone call for years. She had known that it would have to come. "Erm, I'm in the middle of something right now. Could you call back at six-ish?" Lindsay agreed and hung up.

∞

At six o'clock precisely, the doorbell rang, and Sanjay opened it. "Ah, Mr Patel, I presume. Is Carol at home? I have an appointment to see her. She asked me to call around at six o'clock, and here I am on the dot!"

"No, she didn't Mr Lauper. Carol would never do that without discussing it with me first, and as it happens we were just talking about your call this morning. We were expecting a phone call".

"Oh, a phone call? Difficult to do an interview over the phone, and impossible to get a few pictures… May I come in?" When Sanjay turned around to call his wife, the journalist slipped around his back and was in the hall. "What a lovely home you have, Sanjay. May I call you Sanjay?" He took an expensive mobile phone out of his pocket and started taking photographs.

"Hey, stop that! I didn't invite you in, and I certainly didn't give you permission to take photographs inside our home!"

"Your family is the talk of the town, Sanjay. Your public wants to know more. Ah, Carol! Or, should I say, 'Oh, Carol! I am but a fool!'? I thought you told me to call around your house! Anyway, nice to meet you in person at last. Where would you like to do the interview? Are the twins at home?" Carol took the hand that he offered and shook it while Sanjay could hardly believe his eyes.

"Carol, are you going to allow this man to push his way into our home like this?" As he was speaking, Lindsay glided into the front reception room. "Hey!" shouted Sanjay, where do you think you're going? Well, Carol?"

"Sanjay, this is not ideal, but now that he's here, let's just get it over with. We have known that it would happen one day for years… let's just get it out of the way". She took her husband's arm and led him into the room, where Lindsay was taking more photos.

"Mr Lauper, please take a seat at this table", said Carol pulling out a chair at the table in the bay window. "Would you like something to drink?"

"Why yes, thank you. Anything alcoholic: whiskey, wine, beer… the sun has gone under the yardarm, hasn't it?" Sanjay went to the kitchen and returned with a bottle of red Rioja and three glasses.

"We can spare you thirty minutes, Mr Lauper, but then we will be having dinner, and that cannot be delayed", said Carol.

Lindsay clicked a few buttons on his phone, announced the date, the time and 'Interview 1 with Carol and Sanjay Patel at their home in Roath, Cardiff' into it, and laid it on the table between the three of them.

Carol took a phone from her pocket and laid it next to Lindsay's. It was already running.

"Mr Lindsay Lauper, I, Carol Patel, and my husband, Sanjay Patel, do hereby warn you that we expect you to abide by the guidelines laid out by IPSO - the Independent Press Standards Organisation - in all your dealings and interviews with any member of our family. You are expressly forbidden from interviewing our children or taking their photographs without our written consent. Do you understand, Mr Lauper? Please speak for the benefit of the recording".

"Yes, I agree", he said rather dejectedly.

"So, Mr Lauper, what do you want to ask?"

"First of all, could I take a photo of the two of you sitting there?" He took two photos. "Thank you. Whose idea was Celestial Support and the Star Movement groups?"

"I'm not sure", replied Carol. She glanced at Sanjay. "We don't really know. It came from the children, but we don't know which one. It was probably a group decision".

"Not either of you then… or the Williams'?"

"Definitely not ours. I don't know whether Mr or Mrs. Williams suggested it. Why?"

"So, who runs it? Is it run as a charity?"

"The children run it. Well, they're technically children, but they are sixteen years old now. It is a charity, yes. No-one makes any money out of it".

"Is it a registered charity?"

"No, it is the children's idea, and they are too young to set up an official charity. It's a hobby to them".

"It is a very impressive hobby. There are scores of people cooking for them, and scores of homeless people being fed. Some hobby… How long have you lived here, Carol, in this lovely house in Roath?"

Carol looked at Sanjay with a worried expression on her face, but he replied, "Twelve years now".

"Yes, I see, and where are the twins now?"

"They're studying… it's a weekday and there's school tomorrow…"

"Are you planning on turning Celestial Support and the Star Movement groups into a bone fide business, Mr Patel?"

"No", he answered warily, "Carol and I already have full-time occupations. We wouldn't have time for another job…"

"There'd be plenty of money in a charity like Celestial Support and the Star Movement groups, if it were set up correctly though, wouldn't there? I mean, you are a businessman and accountant, and your wife is a solicitor. It could be very lucrative, couldn't it? Very lucrative indeed, I would say".

"I think you have said enough", said Carol, "so, take your nasty insinuations and leave our house".

"OK, I'm leaving, but you haven't heard the last of me yet. I'm onto you. It's disgraceful exploiting children, even your own children, to run an illegal charity to con the generous people of Cardiff into making you rich!"

Sanjay moved towards him, but it was only a gesture. Lindsay picked up his phone, and moved quickly to the front door and left.

"What a horrible man!" said Carol. "I should never have spoken to him in the first place".

"You weren't to know, love, and like you said, we've been waiting for some sort of news about the twins to break for a long time... I just never guessed that it would have taken this kind of twist".

"No, nor me", she agreed. "Call the kids down, let's have dinner, and a couple more bottles of wine".

∞

The following Thursday, Mary popped around to see Carol. "Have you seen this?"

Carol took the newspaper from her friend, let her in, and held it out before her. The front page read:

Cardiff Gazette Exclusive!

Fury as local residents fear exploitation!

Local residents of the STAR area of Splott, Tremorfa,

Adamsdown and Roath were furious last night at the news that the Star Movement could be a scam set up to enrich its founders while using the hapless local homeless as a front for their nefarious activities.

"I can hardly believe it!" growled one angry elderly resident of Titan Road, Splott who wished to remain anonymous.

Carol Patel admitted to our journalist that the Star Movement was not a registered charity, and that it was all the children's idea, something that many people find difficult to believe since the children are only sixteen, but started this work years ago.

"I can't read any more…" said Carol. "That rotten snake of a reporter, and that's a euphemism, has twisted everything and quoted anonymous sources to back it up! It should be against the law… and maybe it is. I'll check later on today".
"It gets worse…". Mary read on:

In the light of the allegations and worries voiced by many, one has to wonder how the four parents of the children could afford two houses in Roath valued at a total in excess of £1,500,000, when their origins were in the noble but humble working class housing estates of Splott and Adamsdown.

"There should be a public enquiry into the finances of these families", said another concerned resident.

"I wonder what the children will make of it", said Mary.

"They know that it's all nonsense", replied Carol, "but I hope that it doesn't affect their relationships with other kids, or their schoolwork. Exams are coming up".

"Yes... they're very sensible kids though. I shouldn't think it will affect them much. Their friends adore them too. I'm concerned, but not worried about them. They'll probably handle it better than we will. I can't help feeling that I've let the side down though. Charity work is not my speciality, but I should have looked into this before. I'll get onto that today as well".

The children found it all very amusing that three kids giving away food to the needy could cause so much fuss. A few days after the newspaper had tried to stir up a controversy, it was all over. Thousands of people wrote letters and posted on social media that they would boycott the Gazette thenceforth, unless a total and unmitigated retraction was given by the editor on the front page where the false allegations had been published.

The ailing newspaper, realising that its bid to cause controversy in order to sell more papers and reverse its fortunes had failed miserably, published a retraction. However, it never fully recovered and when redundancies were announced, Lindsay Lauper was the first to be let go.

Carol rectified the error of not registering the Celestial Support/Star Movement group as a charity, and after an audit of the paperwork that they did have by the Inland Revenue, the case was closed. Nobody ever bothered the trio or their families about their charity again, other than routine government audits, which Sanjay took under his wing. In fact, quite the opposite began to happen. Cardiff City Council began to recognise the good work that the charity was doing. It was even mentioned in the Senedd, the highest government body in Wales. It was Sanjay's ambition to be chosen by the Labour Party to represent the people of his constituency in that august chamber one day.

He knew that he was being considered for the post, and his staff and advisors were helping him to groom his image

When the trio reached the age of nineteen, everyone expected them to go to university since their grades were almost perfect. However, they shocked their family and friends by choosing to stay in a Buddhist monastery in Kathmandu for two years instead. While away, the charity seemed to run itself, because everyone knew what needed to be done, and did what they were capable of doing without being asked. Any organisation would have been proud to have staff as professional and caring as that of the Star Movement.

While the Star trio was away in Kathmandu, nobody heard anything from them, not even their parents, although everybody had been warned what to expect. They were not allowing visitors either.

Nobody outside that monastery ever really found out what went on in there, but it was assumed that they underwent intensive Spiritual Awareness training and Self-Awakening.

10. Remembrance

When the three young adults left the Buddhist monastery in Kathmandu, their parents were outside the gates waiting to meet them. They emerged after their midday meal and were wearing traditional Buddhist monks' and nuns' robes. Their heads were shaven. Alesha and Enaid wore habits of simple white cloth, but Emrys's was of golden yellow - a saffron robe of rough cloth. Emrys was flanked by the nuns, and when they saw their parents, they put their hands together in Namaste.

All four parents had tears in their eyes and wanted to rush forward to hug their children, but something held them back. Something told them that things had changed. They were still their 'children', but not as they had been. They returned the traditional Namaste greeting.

All three of them looked lean, fit and full of vital energy. Something had changed about them, but it was difficult to say what. When the traditional Namaste greeting was over, the three devotees dashed to their parents and hugged them. There was no lack of warmth from any of them towards any of the adults, and that brought sighs, and tears, of relief.

"We were frightened that you would emerge aloof, and not want to talk to us any more", blurted out Carol. "You look so serene, so powerful, so much in control".

"We were only taught how to release our innate selves", replied Alesha. "We were not 'taught' anything as such. It wasn't like school, where you learn maths, or English, or chemistry. We were shown… and encouraged to release ourselves from the constraints that society imposes on each of its members. In essence, we were shown, allowed, and encouraged to be free".

The parents looked, and genuinely were, very proud.

"You look fantastic!" said Sanjay. "Absolutely at the peak of fitness…"

"Positively glowing with energy…" added Mary.

"We were not only encouraged to free our minds", said Enaid, "we also studied Kung Fu. We are more mentally and physically fit than we have ever been in our lives".

"It is all calm and peaceful within those gates", said Emrys. "The test now is to see whether we can carry that peacefulness everywhere we go within us, and project it outwards. The goal is for society to benefit from what we had the privilege to learn from the teacher monks within those walls".

"You do look, er… fabulous, all of you. Look, we've hired a car - it's even got Aircon - and we have rooms in the Dom Himalaya!" When the devotees looked unimpressed, Jonathan added, "It's an expensive hotel in the centre of the city. So, jump in, and let's get out of this dust and heat".

∞

The devotees were shown their rooms, and it was arranged that they would meet within ninety minutes in the hotel gardens. Everyone wanted a shower and to change their clothes. The parents had never known such a dusty environment. It was mostly caused by the proliferation of construction sites, unpaved roads, and excavation work, but the trio were used to it, and were wearing clothing more suitable to their surroundings.

The trio emerged from the hotel on time, and dressed in Western clothing. Their parents had provided the outfits, and they were a little baggy, but they had been wondering whether the kasaya that they had previously worn were to be permanent attire or just uniforms for inside the monastery.

"Sorry about the clothes. We, Mary and I, went off the sizes that you were before you came here, then we added a bit. We didn't expect you to lose weight".

"Don't worry about it, Mum", soothed Alesha. "We haven't actually lost any weight. We have lost our puppy fat, and gained muscle. I think you'll find that we have gained a few pounds".

"Muscle is denser than fat, Mum", added Emrys.

"Yes, of course it is. Anyway, you all look like film stars! Are you hungry? What do you fancy to eat?"

"Well, we don't eat meat or fish any longer… so…" Emrys paused for a moment, and then continued, "we'll have soup and bread to start, a vegetable biryani, lassi, and fruit of the day to finish, please… No, wait… we have all missed a coffee! So, a real black coffee made with coffee beans, and a fruit cake and ice cream to finish, please!"

The three friends all smiled at once. They obviously relished the thought.

Perhaps they missed that in the monastery thought Sanjay, *I wasn't expecting desire.*

"It isn't desire, Dad", said Alesha, "but everyone has preferences. We are very pleased to see our beloved parents , but you were unavailable in the monastery. So was coffee. That is not to put you and coffee on an equal footing, it's just an analogy".

"There is nothing wrong with being happy to have the opportunity to see one's family or friends… or coffee", said Enaid. "They are facts, not comparisons… apples and pears, stairs and steeples".

Jonathan got the joke and smiled, but it seemed to pass the others by. He was rewarded with a smile from the three graduates.

During the meal the conversation was joyful, but a little restrained. The parents were curious about what their offspring had learned, or undergone. They had had absolutely no contact with their children for two years. It wasn't like when children go to university, but phone home every weekend, or send emails asking for money. They hadn't even come home for Christmas or New Year. There had been absolutely zero contact for two years, and they were naturally very curious. On the other hand, the trio did not offer any information, but were still responsive to questions. The evening was extremely enjoyable and everyone went to bed with a smile on their face.

When they checked out to fly home a few days later, the parents were surprised to find on their bill that two of the rooms assigned to the trio had been given up on the first day. They had shared to save costs, not rather than be alone.

∞

The three received a very similar reception from their friends and former colleagues back in Cardiff. Only the twins' paternal grandparents seemed to be completely comfortable with what they were, or had blossomed into. For they could understand that the three were still the same people that they had always been, but they had 'metamorphosed'. Just as a caterpillar becomes a butterfly or moth, though it is the same creature; a 'good runner' at school can become an Olympic athlete; or a pupil with an interest in words can become a famous writer. They settled into the new regime easily. They were prepared to accept the trio for what they really were – bodhisattvas".

They were even tempted to worship them, something that the trio understood, and accepted, but discouraged with supreme grace.

They experienced all shades of attention from their Welsh friends from affection to adulation, and they treated everyone that they met with equanimity. Nobody was above or below - everyone was equal. As Siddhartha explained to his daughter-in-law on one occasion, Buddhists acknowledge the spark of life in all living beings as a token that Spirit resides within them - be they good or bad individuals - much as a soldier salutes the badge of office that an officer wears not the person wearing it.

It was an analogy that Carol found extremely helpful, and she used it often when talking about Buddhism and the trio.

The parents were surprised to see no reaction from their children when they proudly showed them how well their charity was doing.

"Thank you all for taking care of our homeless, but it is not a surprise to us", said Enaid at a family gathering one evening. "We knew that you were 'taking care of business', so to speak. It was not a concern to us. Not only that, but we were frequently here… Not to check up - there was no need - but to give you energy on those days when times got tough. We were absent in body, but present in mind".

It was another of those slightly quirky expressions that they often used. It seemed to give them pleasure.

"We have been working in many spheres", said Alesha. "The Star Project, as it will be henceforth known exists in more localities than just Cardiff. Homelessness is a global concern. Billions of people are less than twelve months from eviction, and most of those are only months away. Almost any working person is potentially at risk of losing their job, missing the rent or mortgage payments, and being evicted. Tenants' rights are being eroded quickly, and the situation will not get better before it gets worse. We need to support people who are at risk, and those who are trying to help".

"Star Projects are being, have been, or will be started all over the world".

"And even further afield," added Emrys, "for the obscenity of homelessness is not confined only to Earth".

Their parents looked as if a car had just crashed through the living room wall, but the trio was unperturbed. It was The Truth', and The Truth can only hurt those who don't want to hear it.

∞

One Sunday afternoon when the two families were enjoying a barbecue of fruit, vegetables and unleavened bread wrapped around sticks, Alesha addressed the group. "We have been aware for some time how curious you all are about what we learned in Kathmandu. We have decided that we can tell you some things, but we will have to be careful what we reveal and when".

Emrys picked the thread up. "You are all on a similar level Spiritually, which makes our desire to reveal what happened easier, but I trust that you will understand, and not take offence…" he said, nodding at his sister, "that we have to reveal Truths gradually, and only to those who will understand them. It is quite clear that it is no use trying to teach Quantum Mechanics to a child who does not yet understand even the basic principles of physics".

The parents understood, but couldn't help feeling a little put out.

"It really isn't an insult", added Alesha, "please don't take it as one. Would you go to university to study advanced Russian literature, without having studied Russian first?" It was a rhetorical question, but she saw that the penny had dropped.

Enaid got to her feet, walking, stopping for brief pauses and gesticulating as she spoke. "We have never mentioned it before, but since the age of five, the three of us have known that we knew each other in different lives. We could even remember some of the things we did.

"We learned how to channel those snippets of knowledge in Kathmandu in such a way, and with such focus , that we now remember that past live, and the intervening decades before we were reborn… chose to be reborn… with you.

"Emrys was my father. His name was William. Willy for short. Alesha was my mother, Willy's wife, Sarah, and I was Becky. We lived not far from here on a hill near Brecon, where Willy was a sheep farmer. We had a lovely dog, called Kiddy, that you may see with us sometimes, and Emrys made a special friend of a huge Siberian tiger called Gāng Zhǎo or Steel Claws whom we all adore as well.

"The cottage is still there, but it is a Spiritualist Church and community centre now.

"Sarah died first. Willy died about fifteen years later, and I followed not long after that. We spent a relatively short term in what you might call Heaven, but others call Annwn, preparing for our next visit to Earth, and here we are".

"That's amazing!" said Sanjay after a minute or so of stunned silence. "But why did you come to us? If you are able to tell us, of course".

"That is a simple question, but the full answer would be complex. The simple explanation is that we decided that we wanted to achieve certain goals, and you were able to provide the correct opportunities for us to be successful. We had a chat with you: you agreed to our proposal and we were born".

"So, why did your sister have to die, Enaid? Was that part of a plan too?" asked Jonathan.

"Yes. Ceridwen needed to be reborn for a short while for her own purposes. She asked to 'tag along' because she didn't want 'her new parents' to be totally bereft. You still had me, which softened the blow, did it not? You and Mum agreed to her proposal too.

"The easiest way of looking at it is to see this planet as a university. A Soul wants to learn a certain lesson, so chooses a course, is reborn, and the course begins. We are all studying something. Some lessons can only be learnt when the Soul has a body. It is more practical. Trying to learn the same lesson without a body would be too academic".

"What is your purpose here?" asked Carol. "Am I allowed to ask?"

"You may ask any question that bothers you, Mum", replied Alesha, "but we cannot always give you meaningful answers… not ones that you would immediately understand, as we said before. The fact is that we discussed our purpose with you before we were born to you, but you have chosen not to remember the details, or you are not able to. If I revealed everything to you, wouldn't that be like going against your wishes or forcing you to learn something that you are not yet ready for?

"Having said that, look around you. Analyse what you see, what has happened, what you think and what you dream. Read. Read Spiritual texts. Knock, and the door will be opened. Everything is available for you, everything can be yours, if you want it enough. Study, and when the student is ready, the teacher will appear. Do not worry that your progress is too slow, you have all the time in the world… in all the very universes and multiverses … all of them! Life, with or without a body is not a race. Everyone will succeed eventually

"Do not worry! Everything will be as you intended".

"Do you remember everything about your previous life on Earth and your stay in Heaven?" asked Sanjay.

"We remember everything, or can remember everything. Not everything is in the front of our minds, but every event can be retrieved, relived, studied and learned from. This facility is not only available to us though. Everyone has this ability, it is just that so few people know about it. So few people understand what they are capable of and even fewer people can be bothered to learn. Learning that is just about the most popular course on this planet."

"How do most people go about obtaining this knowledge, if it is the most popular course on the planet?"

"Unfortunately, in the worst, most wasteful way possible. By trial and error. They just hope for the best. They have to learn to plan to succeed. Compassion and co-operation are the keys to success that most people are looking for, but cannot find. The answers are staring them in the face, but greed, distrust and avarice cloud their vision.

"It is like that old anecdote. A stranger asks a local how to get to a place, and the local replies that if he wanted to go there, he wouldn't start from here. People want to elbow their way into a comfortable financial lifestyle before they consider their Spiritual well-being. That is the wrong place to start from. People can't see this. They can't see the wood for the trees.

"People grab the money. They work hard for, and worry about, money and status to such an extent that it makes them ill and miserable, but they cannot see that if they put a small fraction of that time and effort into their Spiritual well-being, then they could have anything they desired".

"My parents call you bodhisattvas", said Sanjay. "Are you?"

"We know their feelings", replied Emrys. "It is an honour for us that they think that of us. Siddhartha and Tara are very Spiritual beings, and we spend a lot of time with them. We cannot contradict the title they have given us for it is an accurate description in the Buddhist culture… and we are committed to The Truth. However, it is not a term that we would use to describe ourselves. We think that it is putting us on too high a pedestal ".

"You mean that it embarrasses you?" smiled Carol.

"Yes!" they all replied at once.

∞

Sanjay's parents were growing increasingly infirm, but so wanted to see 'the children'. They requested of them that they visit them in their kasaya. The trio was pleased to comply, and walked to their grandparents' house one afternoon. A group of youths mistook them for Hari Krishnas, and mocked them, but it was like water off a duck's back and the bored teenagers soon stopped their harassment.

It had become a custom long before for the three initiates to call Sanjay's parents by their first names. Tara pushed the button to allow them access to the flat above the shop that they had lived in for more than sixty years.

"Good afternoon, Tara, Siddhartha!" they exclaimed in unison as they entered the flat. They hugged Tara when she opened the upstairs door, and then went over to Siddhartha who was seated on an armchair in the bay window so that he could look out over the street before the shop. In his mind, he was still working, but as security surveillance.

"It is so nice to be able to touch you both again", said Alesha. There was little need to talk. They had been in regular contact since they had left for Kathmandu, and their aspirations were in perfect harmony. They only had to sit together and experience each other's presence. Tara had prepared some delicacies in their honour, and made tea. They ate and drank quietly, but it was like a swan on a pond - no apparent action, but lots going on out of sight.

Siddhartha and Tara revered their grandchildren and their friend, and those three had the utmost respect for their elderly friends.

"You look magnificent!" he said with tears in his eyes. "I never dreamt that I would see such a sight again, and you are family - all of you

- even you, my dear, Gāng Zhǎo".

11. The Star Project

"We want to run an idea past you before we put it to the Star Attendants", said Alesha to her parents. The Board of Directors contained only members of the family, but they practised an open management style that allowed anyone who helped to have a say.

"We have never explained why we gave it that name. We reckoned that you would assume it derived from Seren's names meaning 'star' in English. In a way, it does, but there is much more behind it too. A star is a guiding light, and we want our charity to be a guiding light for mankind. People must learn to look after one another again, as they did for millions of years before society was fragmented, and eventually individualised. Members of a village used to take care of each other. They helped look after children, the old and the sick. Nowadays, people don't usually know their neighbours' names, and see their family only on a weekly or even monthly basis rather than every day.

"There are forces at work that this splintered model of society suits. It isolates people, generating loneliness, distrust and fear. This in turn makes people easier to control. Frightened, isolated, lonely people are desperate for help and protection, and the state steps in to offer it.

"Therefore, whoever runs the state exerts this power over its population. Heaven help the people of any state that elects villains. I think that you can see what I am saying.

"In fact, homelessness is a result of this kind of fractured social structure. Could you imagine a homeless person sleeping in a tent on the streets of the village that he or she was born in? No! It is an absurd thought! Yet look at the streets of the world's major cities. Even in the West with all its money, power and might.

"The world has abandoned these people, and yet they are desperate for a guiding light. We want to be a part of the movement that supplies that guidance. There are many organisations trying to alleviate the problem, but they often need help too. We will be there for them as well.

"You have probably often heard Emrys mention a tiger, Gāng Zhǎo, or Steel Claws , in English. He answers to both names now. He's become quite the polyglot these days, haven't you , my friend? Anyway, we propose to use an image of him emerging from the jungle at night with a star in the sky before him leading him on as our logo". Saying this, Emrys bent over and patted his tiger friend's head. He purred loudly in reply.

"You might like to know a little about Gāng Zhǎo, smiled Emrys. "Before we were born to you, a little more than two decades ago, we were involved with rescuing a few Siberian tigers from poachers on the Chinese - North Korean border. Gāng Zhǎo was not one of the rescue tigers, he had already been killed, but he was very friendly with a pregnant female there. I stayed with them when they escaped into the jungle, and was present at the birth of the She's three cubs. Gāng Zhǎo has visited me on and off ever since.

"I don't think that any of you have been aware of his presence, have you?" Sanjay said that he wasn't sure but the others hadn't. Well, here he is, all three and a half metres of him!" Emrys didn't have to bend to stroke him as Gāng had stood up, and the two nuns beamed with affection for the big cat. Sanjay confirmed that he could see an indistinguishable blur, and Mary said that she felt a 'powerful presence '.

"That's Gāng Zhǎo", said Emrys, "He's one hundred percent muscle, and most of it is heart! Aren't you, old boy?" he said, smiling at his own joke. The big cat purred like a well-tuned engine, but not everyone could hear him returning the affection that he was receiving". We have also composed a refrain to go with the logo, a sort of motto, but we may alter it. I would like to give Gāng Zhǎo a mention in it, because he has been such an inspiration to us, but it is perhaps too self-indulgent, since people don't know his story. Let me know what you think.

> In the cosmos where energies are rife,
> "We are the Eternal Star Life,"
> Whispered the spirits in cosmic glee,
> Dancing through the celestial sea,
> Guiding us to realms beyond strife.

"I think it's really lovely", said Mary full of pride. Carol agreed, and they all gave a short round of applause.

"Thank you, thank you! You are too kind", he said smiling. The three gave Namaste, and it was returned to them. "As I mentioned in passing before, homelessness is not a problem that affects only Cardiff, only Wales or the UK, or indeed only this planet. Other planets similar in rank, and below, also suffer from the lack of social, community compassion that creates it. Our task, mine and my sisters' is to organise, or just help, in some cases, as many homelessness projects as we can in the time that we have.

"This means that our Star Project in Cardiff is going to need a Board of Directors and a Steering Committee that does not include us. We think that you four should take on the task of reorganising the movement so that it runs smoothly by taking on others to supplement the help that you have time to give. You are more than qualified to set this up without our help. Indeed, you are better off without us, as we are not au fait with the laws and regulations that affect the running of such a charity. Look at the mess we got you into when we set it up".

"That's not fair", said Carol, "You are being too harsh on yourselves! You were only children back then. You couldn't have known. It is we who should have known better and done something... especially me!"

"That is very generous of you, Mum, but the law of governments really isn't our forte and never will be.

"Back up a minute", said Jonathan. "You said '...in the time that we have left'. What does that mean? You are only in your early twenties. You probably have fifty or sixty years left... or are you leaving again?"

Emrys looked at Enaid. "We are not at liberty to give precise details on that subject, Dad. For the time being, suffice it to say that we will be involved with other Star Projects in other localities, and so will have to leave for periods of indeterminate lengths of time every now and then. However, we will be able to phone you this time. You hinted at 'death', but I hope that you all know in your hearts by now that that concept is false. It is only another form of going away, and contact is still available. More so, in fact, than if we were to be even in another city in Wales. We know when we will return to Annwn, but it is better that you do not, just like most other parents on The Surface of this planet".

"You often refer to Heaven as Annwn, and hint that it is underground. Why do you do that?" asked Mary.

Enaid continued. "The ancient Celts of Britain believed that Heaven was underground, and called it Annwn. When the early Christians arrived here, they were horrified that the locals were worshipping beings that lived underground, since to them, Heaven, where God lived was in the sky, and Hell, where Satan lived was underground. They therefore thought of them as Devil-worshippers. In fact, Christianity was the outlier, because many world religions had the Afterlife as underground or in the sea. To them, Heaven and Hell were in the same place. Hell was just on the wrong side of the tracks. Christianity created a two, or even three tier system if you include Limbo".

"In fact", said Emrys, "the peoples living in the Paektu Mountain Range, where Gāng Zhǎo met his end on Earth, have also believed for centuries that their Heaven is under their mountains. Many still do".

"And why not?", said Alesha. "If it is easier for you to conceptualise where we go when we pass away on Earth as a place, then there is no harm in that. Call it whatever you like, it won't change reality, and it won't harm anyone either. Unless you try to force your beliefs on others like the early Roman Christians did on the Celts, and, missionaries have been doing to other native tribes for the last two millennia".

"Agreed. The World is beginning to realise its mistakes of the past, but don't Buddhists believe in Seven Planes?" asked Jonathan.

"Yes, but they are gradations of resonance, frequency or harmony, not strata between the clouds and somewhere under the topsoil", continued Alesha. Sanjay was nodding. His parents had taught him this all his life. "Every Soul vibrates within a certain bandwidth. This frequency is an indication of that person's Spirituality. The higher, the more evolved.

"This concept of higher and lower is probably where the Christian translators became confused. Thinking that it referred to actual height and depth. Not Christ, of course. He knew better, but the know-nothings who came after him thought that they knew what he had been talking about. Anyway, the Seven Planes… we all gravitate to the Plane that we feel most at home on, but can move freely from one to the other at any time.

"There is an analogy that often helps. If your idea of dining out is going to a local Indian or Chinese restaurant, would you feel comfortable dining at the Ritz? Probably not, but you could go there if you wanted to. Nevertheless, you might feel happy going to a posh local three-star restaurant once a year to celebrate an anniversary. It's the same with pubs. Do you like to have a pint with your mates in the pub down the bottom of the street, where there might be the occasional argument over a football match, or would you prefer to have a cocktail in a five-star hotel where no-one talks to anyone they don't know?

"Reality is not as rigid as is commonly believed in the West. There is no Heaven and Hell; people do not go to one or the other. People drift to where they feel most comfortable, because their vibrations are in synchronisation. It is as simple as that… Most of the facts of life are really simple. It is Man that has said that they are complicated, so that normal people think that they need a priest to guide them, when in reality that priest knows only what his superiors have told him, and those superiors are wealthy, and have a vested interest in maintaining the status quo.

"To put it simply, the major religions of the world have been hijacked by the rich in order to control the masses… and that state of affairs has to be changed. However, one step at a time. Our focus is on the homeless. Other forces are at work remedying the immense damage that state organised religions have done. So many billions of Souls have been thwarted in their search for Enlightenment. It really is a crying shame, but all things will be well.

"That is enough of our explanations of the past, and their hangover into the present, although the pendulum seems to be swinging back into the realm of reality and common sense. Attendance at state churches has dwindled in proportion to the success that Spirit has had in showing people that they don't have to be frightened of a wrathful God. That Being or Entity does not exist and never did, He… She, or It was created solely to control the ignorant masses… to make them more pliable… to make them more likely to do their bosses' bidding. It is an evil that has been perpetuated on mankind, and for which countless hypocrites have paid penance, and still are, by way of Karma".

It was clear that Alesha and her fellows felt very strongly on this subject, but they collectively decided that enough had been said at that time. Emrys changed the subject. "So, dear parents, do you think that you will be able to take on the directorship of the Star Project, even if it is only long enough to put it on a secure, legal footing and elect others to run it?"

∞

"And so," said Enaid from the stage in a large, local former church where they were holding the meeting of Star Attendants, "that is the future that Emrys, Alesha and I propose for the Star Project. To recapitulate, our parents will help you organise a secret ballot to elect five more members to sit on the Project's Board of Directors, and then those nine will elect a Chair who has a casting vote should the need arise. Your charity organisation will be called the Star Project Cardiff, the SPC, and will have Cardiff as its sphere of interest. One day, if the situation calls for it, you may decide to subdivide it into The Star Project Cardiff

North, South, East and West, but other towns will have their own Boards, and their own areas of concern. Again, one day, you may establish a super Board, calling it The Star Project Wales, and then even SPUK. Who knows? That my friends will be up to you.

"At this point in time, I would like to call our parents, Sanjay, Carol, Jonathan and Mary up onto the platform, so that the few who might not know them can see them, and then we will have a question and answer open forum. Please direct your questions to a specific responder or group. However, first of all, will you please give a warm welcome to our parents? Please come up here". A groundswell of clapping and cheering accompanied the four directors as they mounted the stage, waved and took their seats. Emrys took it upon himself to be the Master of Ceremonies, Gāng Zhǎo lying watchfully over the assembled crowd at his feet, and a lively discussion ensued. Whether anyone noticed him or not, no-one ever said, but the odds were that someone there must have been aware of the tiger's presence.

"Before we continue with the debate", he added almost as an aside, "I would like to suggest a logo and a refrain for the charity. You don't have to accept them, the elected Board will deal with that in due course, I just want to show our efforts to you now. Sisters, please". Alesha and Enaid stepped forward. One was holding a poster of Gāng Zhǎo emerging from dense undergrowth being guided by a bright star, and the other held a poster with their Limerick in large letters.

The series of questions that drew the most attention centred on why the trio was leaving the organisation to its own devices. Alesha assured them that they were not abandoning them, but that they needed to release more time to help establish similar groups elsewhere, but she did not give as much detail as they had given their parents before. It brought a collective sigh of relief and a round of applause from the attendees.

The local press was represented in the hall, and public relations handouts were available for anyone who wanted to report on the meeting in their TV or radio channels, or even on their blogs, websites and social media pages. The meeting was a massive success, and the reporting was all favourable in varying degrees. The meeting was on the local evening news, and the following day there were reports in the local newspapers, and blogs. Several days later, it even got a small mention in the national media, and the charity realised that it would need to handle PR carefully.

Over the following week, five more board members were elected. Those nine chose Mary as chairwoman.

"Me?" she responded in her opening address. "I can hardly believe it. I am very flattered by your confidence in me, and I will do my utmost to do the right thing for the homeless, our charity, and our members… although you will have to give me some time to learn how to do that". She was genuinely surprised that they had elected her, as she was probably the most retiring person on the Board, but then perhaps that was why. Carol became the legal adviser, Sanjay the finance officer. Other responsibilities were assigned to newer members.

The trio was delighted with the way things had gone, and so was everyone else.

12. Unforeseen Developments

The immediate result of all the extra publicity following the charity meeting was a vast increase in donations. During the first seven days of the new regime, The Star Project Cardiff received donations equivalent to those of an average six-month period. Many local firms wanted it to be known that they supported the homeless project. Gail, the new Board Member responsible for fund-raising was doing a fantastic job. She and a team of volunteers went from shop to shop, and business to business asking for donations, while others manned a few mobile phones.

It resembled an American presidential fund-raising campaign, which was what Gail said she had based her strategy upon. She even persuaded two local companies to buy them a beef burger style van each. They didn't have cooking facilities, but they did have a warm and a cold storage container that was run from the main engine. This allowed them to collect meals from Star Chefs, and deliver them to drop-off points. They were also useful for a new phenomenon, which was also due to Gail's ingenuity.

Restaurants were donating cooked food that they could not keep overnight, which meant that there were usually high-quality midnight meals available.

This prompted them to move to a recyclable cardboard meal box and discontinue the polystyrene containers, which they had never been comfortable using. Some had worried that shoppers and midnight revellers would try to take advantage of the free or cheap food because it was of such high quality, but volunteers reported very little abuse by the non-homeless. Likewise, some restaurateurs had protested that their clients might stop paying for food from them, if they could get the same food from the charity, but this fear proved to be unfounded as well.

Some restaurants even reported increased sales because people found out that they were supporting the SPC.

It seemed that everybody wanted to be associated with the Project.

"Should we offer branding opportunities?" asked Gail at one Board meeting. "We are receiving so many requests from companies and organisations that want to have their name associated with ours".

"Oh, I don't know about that", objected Tim, who dealt with public relations. "I'm worried that it would create negative PR to have business names plastered all over our vans and containers. These companies didn't give two hoots about the homeless before, but want to jump on the bandwagon now. I don't like it… not one little bit".

"The Chair notes your objection, Tim. Let it be minuted", said Mary. "Let's discuss the matter for thirty minutes, and then put it to a vote". People checked the time.

"From a fund-raising standpoint", said Gail, "it makes perfect sense, but I do understand Tim's concerns. Think about how much businesses would be willing to pay though. We are not struggling for cash right now, but this flurry of attention could die down in a few months, and then what?"

"Objection!" said Tim. "It is my job not to let the amount of attention fade, and I think that my team is doing a grand job. Are there any complaints? If so, let's hear them now!"

"There have been no complaints, Tim. None that I have heard", soothed Mary.

"No, none, and I am not saying that there have been or will be any", said Gail. "You and your team, Tim, are doing a fantastic job… No-one is saying otherwise. I just want to point out that there is a ton of extra cash out there and people are willing to give it to us. It is our job on this board to imagine all possibilities and devise tactics to deal with them, right? Well, for the sake of a little discrete branding, we could pay our Star chefs more, and, or, we could lend money to other start-up Star Projects - like, say, Barry - to help them get going"

"How would Cardiff donors feel if they knew that their money was being spent in Barry?" asked Huw, who had responsibility for acquiring food and meals.

"I don't know", said Gail with some exasperation in her voice, "we would have to find out. Perhaps, do a sample survey. It really isn't difficult. Anyway, the money would come back to us… it would only be a short-term loan. That is possible, isn't it, Sanjay?"

"Yes. I don't see why not. Would charging interest be illegal, Carol?"

"I think it might be, but I'll find out". She made a note on her phone's calendar.

"We don't have to charge interest though, do we? We are a charity that has been given free money… we don't have to behave like a bank! All I am suggesting is that we use sponsorship to increase the value of the services that we provide at no extra cost to ourselves. It is a win-win situation!"

And so it went on. They voted to extend the original thirty minutes with another thirty, and then held the vote.

"The motion to apply the discrete branding logos of donors of cash, goods or services with a total value in excess of £5,000 has been carried. Branding will be allowed subject to this Board's approval in each case", said Mary. "Right, if no-one has anything else to say for the good of the charity, I vote that we call the meeting to a close and go out for something to eat". They often went for a meal or a drink after a late evening Board Meeting, and often those informal social gatherings were an excellent source of opinion.

While Carol drove, Sanjay informed the trio over a video link about what had transpired at the meeting. They approved, not they would have tried to interfere if they had not. They had other fish to fry.

∞

Gail, and most of the Board, was delighted with the decision. She and her team leapt at the new challenge with renewed enthusiasm. They phoned around the companies on a list that Gail had kept of those that had expressed a wish to donate 'a little extra' if their company names were used on the SPC's goods. The first to sign up was a local chain of fast food outlets. They donated £10,000 to have the sole right to supply the charity with serviettes to supply with their meal boxes. They provided a minimum of 15,000 good quality serviettes a month with their logo in one corner. It read: 'Beefy Burgers is proud to support The Star Project Cardiff', and the quality of the tissues was triple what they had been buying with donated cash before the vote.

Gail used the example to vindicate what she had said at that auspicious board meeting.

Not to be outdone by their archrival, another fast food chain struck a similar deal, but supplied the fast-food boxes. They looked remarkably like their own boxes, but did carry The Star Project Cardiff name and logo prominently as well.

One morning, Gail was almost struck dumb by a phone call she received.

"Good morning! Gail here from The Star Project Cardiff. How may I help you?"

"Good morning, Gail. I'm fine and I hope that you are too. My name is Gareth Lloyd of Lloyd, Lloyd and Jenkins Solicitors, and I think that I am going to make your week. I have been instructed by a client, who is very impressed by the good works that your SPC is doing, to make you a charitable donation - a rather substantial donation. Unfortunately, my client has asked to remain nameless even to you until you accept their offer, and even then you will not be at liberty to reveal it to the general public".

"OK", she replied hesitantly, but it is not my SPC. You do understand that, and so does your client, right?"

"Yes, of course, I was speaking rather loosely. We are aware of the structure of the charity. Would you be prepared to accept the donation of a disused church?"

"A building?" she blurted out embarrassing herself with the volume of her question.

"Yes, churches usually do fall under that category", he chuckled.

"You want to give us a church?"

"My client does, yes. If you are amenable to the proposition, perhaps I could see you in my office on St. Mary Street tomorrow morning. Would eleven-thirty be convenient. I realise that you might want to consult with your colleagues first".

"Yes. I will be there. Gareth. See you tomorrow".

Gail phoned Mary immediately. Mary phoned around, and an hour later, Gail was given authority to collect the details from the solicitor the following day.

∞

Gail arrived at the office punctually looking slightly smarter than she usually did, her normal job not calling for more than jeans and a T-shirt.

"Good morning, Gail. May I call you Gail?"

"Certainly".

"Thank you. Please take a seat. My name is Gareth Lloyd. Please call me Gareth. Would you like tea or coffee and a custard slice? I'm having one. I have a soft spot for custard slices, but my doctor has warned me not to have more than one a day for five days a week". He rubbed his paunch through his grey, pin-striped suit. Gareth was in his mid-fifties, amiable and balding. Gail, who was about ten years younger, took an immediate liking to him and looked at his ring-finger automatically. He wore a gold ring. She was not checking out of a romantic interest, she was happily married; it was just an automatic response.

"OK, black coffee, no sugar and a slice. Thank you".

"Excellent! One doesn't feel so guilty indulging in company, does one?" He phoned the order through to his secretary, and she appeared a few minutes later with a tray. Gareth passed Gail a cup and saucer and a custard slice on a small plate with a cake fork. "I have a very pleasant task to perform today… Sad to say that not every day is so agreeable. Now, down to business. My client, who shall remain nameless, has quite a large property portfolio and is seeking to liquidate some of them. Obviously, that normally means selling them, but on this occasion, is willing to donate one to your charity. If you accept the offer there are some caveats, not all of which are imposed by my client. The gift is dependent on your acceptance of these clauses".

"I can't, I mean we can't say yea or nay until we know what they are".

"No, quite. They are quite straightforward. The client insists that you do not resell the property for one hundred years, or the deeds will be forfeit to them, and, you may not erase the wording on the outside or inside of the building. That is law anyway since the property is a listed building".

"That sounds perfectly reasonable, but I have to take details back to our Board for a group decision.

∞

"You are going to love this", said Gail, as she handed each member of the Board a large manilla envelope.

"A church!?" exclaimed Jonathan. "Someone wants to give us a church?"

"Yes", said Gail proudly. "A two-hundred-year old Tabernacle complete with two-hundred and fifty-seven graves and headstones!" she grinned. The expressions on the faces of the Board members as they read through the literature and examined the photos was a picture in itself, and she couldn't help smiling to herself. "It's rather run down, and can't be demolished because it is a listed building. It ran out of congregation twenty years ago, and the only life there now is pigeons and rats. The local residents have been complaining for years. They are probably offering it to us because it's a white elephant. It is an eyesore, dangerous, and smelly; it costs too much to stop it falling down - see the scaffolding? - and yet there is nothing they can do with it. If we do it up and try to resell it, the property would revert to the current owner. So, it's a gift, but it is not given purely out of philanthropy".

"Understood, Gail. Thank you. Well, what do we think?"

"The rates for a property like this within walking distance of the city centre must be horrendous!" said one member.

"Yes, like I said, this is not a purely philanthropic gesture, but I still think that we can make good use of it", said Gail. "Anyway, we have seven days to make up our minds. After that, they may accept any offer that they may receive from other parties. I suggest that we all do our own research and meet back here in three days to pool our findings and make a final decision". Gail's motion was accepted unanimously.

∞

At the meeting, it was clear that most people had liked the idea of accepting the white elephant Tabernacle, but were worried about the costs.

"I took a builder around the church the other day", said Gail handing out sheets of paper to each member. "These are his findings.

"The Tabernacle. Starting at the top. It will need a new roof, but the roof timbers are sound. The slate is Welsh, so very expensive, but most of it is salvageable, and we can patch it with second hand slates. The walls are mostly sound, but parts of the gable end are crumbling and will need repair. The windows are all smashed, and the frames are rotten. The doors are all smashed off their hinges too. No underpinning is required but there is substantial damp and water penetration. It needs re-plastering and a damp course injection. The suspended floor is rotten and dangerous. There is a substantial rodent presence. The dwelling is in a similar state to the Tabernacle.

"It will cost between £500,000 and £750,000 to put it right. We may qualify for a grant to cover part of the costs, and we almost certainly would be granted 'change of use'. It would then be fit for habitation. We could turn it into rooms and a kitchen with a communal dining area, and have a dwelling for a warden or whatever they are called - someone to run the place and maintain order.

"I reckon that we could get the whole project completed and made operational by the use of donors within six months tops - maybe four or five".

Gail glanced around the table, but most people looked glum - worried.

"It's a huge undertaking, Gail, and none of us has any experience in renovation, or building work of any kind…"

"Exactly, Rod! My thoughts exactly. It's too risky", added Tim.

"I won't be of much use to you", said Jonathan. Most people were either pretending to study their papers or were shaking their heads.

"What if I could find an architect, or structural engineer to oversee the job?" asked Gail

"I was just thinking about my Dad", said Carol. "He's retired, but he was a structural engineer. I could ask him whether he could help".

"Good idea, my dear! I'm pretty sure that Dylan would love to get back in the saddle for one final project. It would be a feather in his cap. This opportunity is far too good to pass up lightly. We need to pull out every stop before we turn it down. Offers like this will not come every year. So, you'll ask him tonight, will you, Carol?". She agreed and the mood of the Board was lifted immediately.

∞

Far away, the three initiates were smiling to themselves. They had been following events and were overcome with joy that the SPC had not given up on the first major hurdle that had been placed before them. They were confident now that the charity would go from success to success, because they already knew that Dylan would probably accept the offer to run the renovation of the inner city church and its conversion into a temporary stay hostel for the homeless.

∞

Mary signed the deeds of the Tabernacle accepting ownership on behalf of the charity at the end of the week. That evening, there was a party atmosphere as they made the announcement to the attendees, although Gail had been at work since an hour after it was announced that Dylan had offered to oversee the renovation of the Tabernacle.

'Her builder' offered to repair the brickwork free of charge so long as he could put his signboard on the perimeter wall for the duration of the renovation, and get a permanent mention on a roll of honour inside the building when it was complete. He also suggested a roofing company and a scaffolder that he regularly worked with. They offered to do the job on similar terms.

These companies brought their own experienced employees with them, but Dylan did hire some of the more willing homeless to clear the ground of weeds and move debris into skips, after the city rat-catchers had sanitised the grounds. They were paid the going rate for labourers and were promised priority for a room, if they were still homeless when the building was finished. This was unlikely, since, with a decent wage, they could afford to return to a more normal style of life, despite the ballooning rents being charged in Cardiff and around the country.

Carol handled the charity's legal paperwork regarding the church. She worked closely with Gareth Lloyd, who offered to do the conveyancing free of charge. His company's name was added to the roll of honour although he had not asked for any recognition. Many people adopted the same attitude. The building site workers stopped bringing lunch with them, because local businesses and residents would bring them sandwiches, chips and curries, because they were so grateful that something was being done about the blot on their neighbourhood which they were sure was having a negative affect on their own property prices.

Tim had voiced his concern that the residents near the Tabernacle might object to having thirty-odd homeless people living near them, but this worry never materialised. The removal of the eyesore that had been a risk to their children and local public health had outweighed any such concerns. The boost in property values had been a bonus.

Leaving Annwn

13. Crisis? What Crisis?

As the Tabernacle was nearing completion, and the SPC team were feeling that they had sailed their ship into calmer, easier waters, an article appeared in the South Wales Clarion with the headline: 'SHOCK AS CARDIFF BECOMES NEW UK CAPITAL OF HOMELESS'. The article went on to describe how the success of the SPC had resulted in the homeless from South Wales and the West flocking to Cardiff to seek shelter, and how that would ruin the lives of the good people of Cardiff, which seemed a poor reward for their generosity. 'The road to Hell is paved with good intentions', it warned.

"That takes the icing off the cake and no mistake..." grumbled Tim at a board meeting. "It's a PR disaster! If we don't handle this correctly, we're going to lose much of the local support that we have worked so hard - and for so long to acquire".

"It sounds bad for sure", said Gail hesitatingly, "but I'm not a hundred percent convinced of the allegation. Rod, are you aware of increased queues at the food stations?"

"Very slightly, yes, but that could be seasonal. He pushed a few keys on his laptop to call up a graph and showed it to the others. The X axis represents the days, and the Y axis the number of meals served. As you can see. There has been very little variation this month... just the usual weekend spikes, and we put those down to drunken revellers passing themselves off as homeless to get a free meal before going home".

"So, it could be just conjecture?" asked Mary.

"It could be, but it sounds logical that homeless people would come here, if the conditions here are much better than where they currently are".

"Agreed", said Mary. "It does sound logical, but what do we do about it? We can't suddenly make conditions for the homeless worse! That would go against our raison d'être. Are there any thoughts on the matter?"

"I think that the only real course of action is to extend the Star Project to all major cities, so that the homeless can stay where they are. They would not have any reason to come here then", said Sanjay. "Surely, a homeless Bristolian would rather remain in Bristol than move to Cardiff, where he or she probably wouldn't know anyone?"

The board agreed, but no-one knew how to proceed. "Let's call it a night, and sleep on it" suggested Mary. Since the PR crisis hadn't happened yet, everyone was willing to do as proposed.

However, once home Carol and Mary phoned their offspring to seek advice. They put their parents on video phone and spoke as one through Alesha.

"The situation that the newspaper is talking about has been predicted, but, as you know, it has not happened yet… and it will not happen on a scale that you cannot manage. Everything is going to plan. Right now, literally as we speak, there are many Star Projects being rolled out across the country in order to help the homeless and forestall the backlash that worries you.

"It will not happen. Have faith. Continue with what you are doing. The charity has changed many lives for the better, and will continue to do so. We will not allow the generosity of the people of Cardiff to be a burden to them.

"Listen to Gail. She is receiving, and passing on sound advice. Accept it, if you see fit, but always bear in mind that if your goals are honourable, Spirit will not let you down. We are only a call away. Do not think that we have abandoned you or the SPC. It is the hub of a global institution that will eventually change the way the world treats the homeless. You are at the forefront of a revolution that will have much wider consequences than you are considering at this point in time.

"Do not worry about the future, it is in hand, and running according to plan. Our plan, and your plan, and the plan of everyone involved in the Star Project. We may stumble in the future, but we will not fail. Remember that, and be strong for those others, who want to help but need support, encouragement and guidance in order to do so.

"We are all in this together".

"Where are you now?" asked Carol, speaking as a mother not a colleague.

"We are never far away, Mum", said Alesha, detecting the change of tone in her mother's voice. "Please try never to worry about us. We are working on the Star Project, alleviating the potential problem of Cardiff becoming the homeless capital of the UK. Cardiff will become a beacon, a shining example of how man should behave towards those less fortunate than themselves. We have been working on this for quite some time. You will soon receive news that will put your minds at rest, and stop any backlash from concerned citizens in the Welsh capital. Be patient just a little longer. The press is just selling newspapers. You have nothing to worry about. Go with God". They all performed the Namaste, as had become their custom and closed the link.

That night, the six o'clock city news also reported on the 'impending crisis' that hordes of homeless from 'all over the UK' might descend on Cardiff making it a no-go area for decent local citizens. Carol phoned Mary immediately.

"Mary, were you just watching the news on TV? I know that our kids just told us not to panic and all that, but I think they were also saying that we should handle the charity's affairs as we see fit too, don't you? ... Right! So, I suggest that we put out a press release tomorrow explaining the situation as we see it and proving what we say using our own statistical data. What do you think?"

"I think you're right. Let's try to nip this rabble-rousing in the bud before people start to get spooked, because that could ruin all the good work that so many people have put into the SPC. I'll phone Tim right away, and ask him to prepare a press release with Rod's data that we can all look over and issue tomorrow morning".

"Excellent! Perhaps we should all make a few notes. While you're talking to Tim, I'll send out a group email to the Board".

"Good. Let's get cracking!".

∞

"Did you see that downstairs?" asked one of the Board members as she took her seat at the table. "Scary, isn't it? Whatever next? I don't like the look of it at all"

"Ah, don't worry about it", advised Sanjay. "Just a couple of drunks walking home last night. It happens from time to time. My parents had to put up with it for decades at the shop".

"I'm not so sure, Sanjay", mumbled Tim embarrassed. "They were racist idiots who tormented your parents. There was a lot of that kind of stuff in the Seventies… you know, with the National Front, and the British Party. The people who smashed our front window and daubed 'Keep Cardiff for the residents!' on the wall might not be very bright, but they are probably concerned members of the public".

"Of course, they're members of the public!" retorted Sanjay a little too aggressively. "What else could they be?" Carol patted him on the knee in an effort to calm him down. He acknowledged her concern with a shy glance of remorse. It was not like him to lose his self-control, but racism always had made him see red - even the thought of it, and the memories that it evoked in him from his childhood.

"I'm just saying that they would have had to go home to get the paint, or have taken it to the pub with them - and that's not very likely, is it? This attack, or protest, whatever you want to call it, was planned. As far as I can see, anyway".

"The nasty slogans on my parents' shop were planned too!"

"Yes, but probably by the NF or BP. Who would have organised last night's escapade? Anyway, this is the press release that I wrote last night". He slid copies across the table to everyone.

The Board approved the Press Release after Rod had supplied some statistics about queues at the food stations. He added it to the PR on his computer in graph form and posted it to the SPC blog. It showed an 'inconsequential' increase of three percent, which was within the normal monthly fluctuation. Mary asked that the press release be sent to all local media stations and be posted on each member's own blog and social media sites.

"Is there any other business?" asked Mary.

"I want to propose that we move our office to the Tabernacle. It would make any future attacks far less likely, since it would be manned permanently and around the clock", said Alice, who was in charge of purchases and acquisitions. "I'm not sure how we would stand legally though, what with it being listed and all".

"No. All right. Suggestion noted. Carol, would you look into that, please? One last thing, before we go about our daily duties", she said, "I have informed the insurance company about the vandalism, and they are sending a glazier around this morning to fix the broken window. I have already informed the police and been given a crime number. Anything else?"

"We could use this opportunity to coat the outside wall with anti-graffiti paint. It'll brighten the place up a bit, and make it easier to deal with any future graffiti, should there be any. That's what my parents ended up having to do" suggested Sanjay.

"I'm not sure about whether we would need the landlord's permission for that, Sanjay" said his wife. "I'll check the lease". The remedial work was agreed, pending Carol's reading of the lease, and one of the members was delegated to get photos of the damage. As the meeting closed, voices could be heard outside. Some of the Board went to the window to ascertain the reason for the commotion.

"Would you look at that?" said Rod astounded. "Pickets! Outside our office!"

"At least they're peaceful", said Alice.

"It is still probably unlawful according to recent changes in the laws of obstruction and inconvenience" advised Carol. "I'll inform the police".

When they had walked down from their office on the first floor, they could see the protestors more clearly, and the protestors saw them for the first time. The ringleader urged them to wave their banners and increase the volume of their chant, 'Keep Cardiff for the residents!'. Suddenly, Jonathan spotted a man on the other side of the road filming the event on his mobile phone.

"It's a set-up!" he said to Mary. "Our response is being filmed. This'll be on TikTok and SnapChat later, I bet you".

"You're right", agreed Mary. "Keep calm!" she said to the board members. "We're being filmed, don't do anything you don't want the world to witness. Smile, you're on Candid Camera!"

The police arrived moments later, and moved the protesters on. There was no argument, they just dispersed as if it had been pre-arranged that they should do so. It seemed that the protest, the arrival of the board members and the police was all that the cameraman had wanted. The question was: why?

Jonathan was correct, but the film appeared as an 'eye-witness' account on the six o'clock regional TV news as well as on social media, although the 'contributor' was unidentified.

∞

The initiates returned to Cardiff to stay with their parents the following day. They had not been expected, but it was a very welcome surprise when they appeared in their robes.

"How long will you be staying this time?" asked Carol nervously, not wanting to pry.

"We will be here for the official opening of the Tabernacle Hospice", replied Emrys. "Most of our initial work has been done, and your work will start in earnest soon. We want to be here for that".

She looked at her children with amusement. "You mean that everything that we have done so far was just a trial run?"

"No, Mum!" said Alesha grinning, "not a trial run exactly, but the best is yet to come. Put it that way". Neither Carol nor Sanjay understood, but they knew better than to ask. Their 'children' only ever told them what they wanted them to know.

"Have you decided to wear your robes as everyday clothing now?" she asked.

"We will wear what is most suitable for the occasion, Mum", replied Emrys, "but it seems that our Buddhist robes suit the occasion more often than not these days".

"They do suit you. There is no doubting that. You look 'natural' in them. On you, they are not an affectation - that's what I am trying to say, whereas they seem unsuitable when many Westerners wear them. That sounds awkward..."

"Don't worry, Mum, we know what you mean. Thank you".

The charity community was delighted to see the trio, who found it difficult to get any work done because all of their former close collaborators wanted to know how they were, where they had been, and what they had been doing. They did not have the filter that stopped them asking personal intrusive questions like the parents had. It took days for the excitement around their return subsided. During that time, emails were arriving almost continuously - dozens a day - from Star Projects in cities and towns all over the UK. Some were even coming from abroad, but they all had similar content, and it rang along the lines of:

> 'We heard about your wonderful initiative to help the growing flood of homeless in Cardiff and it inspired us to attempt the same. We were helped initially by three helpful young people from Cardiff who said that they knew you and had worked with you. They were very approachable and knowledgeable. If you see them again, please convey our deepest gratitude to them. Keep our email address, and we hope that you will allow us to seek your advice, if we run into a situation we can't handle - you having so much more experience in these matters. It's funny but we feel that we

know you already. Please keep in touch… Why not start a newsletter and sign us up for it? Greetings, Star Project So-and-So'.

The messages touched the hearts of all the Cardiff team members who heard or read them. A board member answered each email personally, and some of the messages received more than one reply. A warm network of like-minded people was growing not only across the UK, but also Europe and the World.

"Were you the three 'helpful young people' that they all mention?" asked Jonathan, but the only reply that he received was a grin and "We couldn't possibly comment".

∞

The following evening, Sanjay burst into their home in Roath. He was so overflowing with exuberance that he startled Carol and the three initiates who were chatting, while waiting for him to come home for dinner. Jonathan and Mary were also expected any moment and they walked in through the open front door behind him. "I'm glad that you are all here. Come in, come in. Take a seat. I've got something to tell you!

"You know that the Party has been grooming me as a candidate for the Senedd for a while now, don't you? Everybody nodded, and as one guessed what he was going to announce. Well, what I haven't told anyone is that several of those who supported me were becoming a bit flakey because of the protests and the negative press. For a while, they were considering dropping me in favour of Rick Powell. Nevertheless, I was told today that the controversy is now considered a false flag, and so, as of today, I am the official Labour candidate for this constituency at the up-coming Welsh election!

"What do you think of that, kids? Your Dad a Member of the Senedd! Sanjay Patel MS!" Jonathan and Mary applauded, but Carol and the trio were all around him hugging him like a hero".

"That's fantastic, Dad", said Alesha.

"We knew you could do it!" said Emrys, and that made everybody stop and think. While Carol and Mary went for wine, fruit juice and glasses, Sanjay asked, "Did you three have anything to do with this by any chance?"

"We don't know what you mean!" joke-lied Emrys.

"We couldn't possibly comment!" added Alesha.

"What is it?" asked Carol returning.

"Somehow, our kids had a hand in this".

"In what?"

"In my nomination for the Senedd".

"Did you? I mean, there's nothing wrong if you did, but did you?" asked Carol.

"There are hands at work in everything that happens", said Alesha mysteriously. "If our lives are planned by us before we are born, then nothing happens by accident. There is no such thing as coincidence. In that sense, we all had a hand in your nomination because it fitted in with the plan that is unfolding before our very eyes".

"Just imagine what good you could do, initiate or encourage from the highest seat of power in the land" added Emrys. "Which organisation would not want a sympathiser in the government? It is not that we three waved a magic wand today, and you got nominated. It was planned many years ago by all of us in this room and many, many others on both sides of the grave that none of us have ever met.

"The power of Spirit is truly awesome. Very few people in Annwn understand it fully, and almost no-one here on The Surface. The human brain is just incapable of comprehending it. It is just physically inadequate. The hardware is too old fashioned. It's like trying to use a 386 computer to run Windows 11 - it just cannot, even with all the good will in the world. In fact, that is part of the challenge - like a three-legged race - we are hamstrung, but we have done it to ourselves".

"Well, that's taken the wind out of my sales, hasn't it?"

"It shouldn't, Dad. We all, including you, decided years ago that you were the best guy for the job that you have been performing - and will perform. Since you have just cleared the first hurdle, you have proved that we were all right to choose you. Congratulations!"

"Almost any worthwhile achievement is the result of co-operation. People just don't usually achieve outstanding feats alone. They take too much energy - one person doesn't have enough power. It takes more than one battery for a torch to provide a powerful light to illuminate the way ahead".

The group of family and friends sat down to a hearty meal, and told stories and anecdotes until the early hours. The parents went to bed tipsy, but the trio drank only fruit juice. It was the first such gathering that they had had in a long while, and the chance to let their hair down, enjoy life and celebrate Sanjay's appointment was relished by all. They promised each other that they would have to do it more often, since things finally seemed to be going their way both as far as the charity and their personal lives were concerned.

14. Two Ends, and Two Beginnings

"You know that things are going well, don't you, dearest grandparents?" Alesha said to Siddhartha and Tara in the presence of her fellow initiates. "You have played a pivotal rôle in the success of the Star Project, yet you have not received any recognition for your work".

"Thank you for saying that, and thank you for honouring us and our humble home with your visit. Accolades are not for Tara and me. We don't need them. What use is a medal? Or a mention in a newspaper that will be used in a cat litter tray the following day? We have passed those needs by".

"We would have done all that we did and more, just to meet your wonderful friend Gāng Zhǎo", joked Tara, "but seriously, our reward is the privilege that it was to work with you and help the community."

"Yes, we know that you both feel that way. It has been a pleasure to meet, and work with you too".

"We hope that this is the first of many occasions that we will work together, now that our usefulness here is almost at an end".

"So do we. It has been a most enjoyable experience. In a way, it is sad that it is coming to an end, but all things do, eh? Otherwise, nobody would have the time to start anything new. We will meet again, and work together again soon. In the meantime, Peace be with you, and go with God".

"Go with God, our brother and sisters". With that the trio left. They had other friends to visit before the morning was out and the festivities at the church began.

It was to be a busy morning, but then the whole week after the initiates had arrived back had been a blur of activity. Foremost was the completion and handing over of the hospice and the moving of the charity's office from a dingy backstreet to the altogether brighter surroundings of the former church. These two activities occupied most people's time and thoughts. However, the Patel family also had to deal with Sanjay's preparations for the upcoming election.

Completing the Tabernacle was just a question of cosmetics, and moving the office - one of carting furniture, equipment and supplies from one location to the other, but Sanjay's preparations were gruelling. He had assembled a specialist team to help and advise him, but he was starting from scratch.

First, he had to formulate his policies, then write speeches to promote them, and finally, he had to memorise them. He had to fit this around spending hours and hours a day going from house to house campaigning. His Party was confident of a win, but Sanjay wasn't so sure.

Cardiff Central has historically been a stronghold for the Labour Party, so I have a fighting chance, but what if I make a mess of things? he asked himself frequently.

When the day of the handover arrived, he didn't know whether he was coming or going, but he decided to take the day off from politics and let his hair down. The two neighbouring families decided to walk to the church together. Carol's parents would be there earlier to oversee the smooth running of the function, and Sanjay's parents were planning to go by car, if Siddhartha's knees were up to it.

The show started at one o'clock, and sideshows, stalls and caterers had paid to be able to sell their goods and services. The weather was fine and the forecast was good. It was set to be the biggest local event of the year. It was to be better than carnival. Toddlers carried balloons, children were wearing their brightest clothes, and teenagers in love were walking arm in arm. Even the trio looked excited, and it was usually difficult to judge what was going through their minds because nothing seemed to phase them. They took whatever came their way with indifferent equanimity. They always looked as serene as swans.

The atmosphere was fantastic. It was set become a day that the community would talk about for decades

Dylan was the star of the Topping Out Ceremony at the moment when the completed Tabernacle was officially handed over to its charity owners, and rightly so. He and his team had completed the task on time and to a high quality. He saw it as his crowning glory, and when he handed over the keys on stage to rapturous applause, he had tears in his eyes.

"Thank you all very much", he was heard to say. "Obviously, I didn't do it on my own. I had a wonderful team that made my job a pleasure, and an easy one at that. Now, I need a beer. I'm not used to getting applause for just doing my job". He wasn't used to working with a mike either, because the last part was not meant to be heard by the assembly. However, they did hear him, and they reacted with redoubled applause and laughter.

Dylan was lost for words, so he just touched his forelock in salute and left the stage. The crowd loved him as did those who had worked with him over the previous six months. He was a natural born leader of the old school.

"Thank you, Dad", said Carol as he walked past her. "What a guy!"

"I won't keep you long, I promise. I just want to thank everyone who made this Star Project possible… from our neighbours who brought us food and tea, to the contractors who completed the work free of charge!

"Now I will hand you over to our Chairperson, Mary, who wants to say a few words. Brothers and sisters, ladies and gentlemen, Mary!"

The applause started again and she also thanked everyone for the part that they had played, before revealing that the Star Project was now being rolled out across the UK and even further afield. The finale was the announcement of who the first occupants of the hospice would be. Seven of the rooms were to go to people who had worked on the property, and the other twenty-five were chosen by a live lottery. The winners of the free lottery lined up on stage and were also subject to a round of applause.

"And finally, and I really do mean finally, I have a surprise for you. The vast majority of you know who is really behind The Star Project…" - a low-pitched sound of appreciation could be heard - "Yes, The Star Children have agreed to make an appearance. I know that most of you have not seen them for a long time. They have been travelling… establishing other instances of the Star Project all over the UK, Europe and even further afield than that. So, without further ado, I want to leave the stage to the Star Children. Let's hear it for Alesha, Emrys and Enaid - the Star Children, your real benefactors".

They passed Mary as she left the stage. They would have preferred a far less show-bizzy introduction, but they knew why Mary had done it. She wanted to make sure that the triad realised just how much they were respected, and she also wanted to create an atmosphere that encouraged donors to give more. They acknowledged her, and walked out onto the stage, in their robes, to rapturous applause.

They did what they could to dial down the uproar, but that amounted to just standing centre stage and giving Namaste. After several minutes, the pleas for quiet… the shushes won out, and there was silence. Yet still the trio maintained both their silence and their pose.

After a full minute of complete silence, Emrys, flanked by the nuns, spoke.

"Brothers and sisters, you have achieved wondrous things. Look around you, not only in this hospice, but as far as you can see. The effect of your positive actions to help others has inspired people around the whole world to emulate you… Yes, you, people from Cardiff, who probably never thought that people abroad had ever heard of your country let alone a tiny project that you began only a decade ago.

"My sisters and I applaud you", and they clapped for a few seconds and then returned to the Namaste. Gāng Zhǎo flopped on the floor at their feet. Emrys made a point of stooping to pet his friend. A few people in the audience let it be known that they could see the tiger. "Yes, this is our friend, Gāng Zhǎo. He is a Siberian tiger, and he wants you to know that he will always be on the side of those who are on the side of The Star Project, don't you, boy?" There was a chuckle from the crowd.

"We want you to know that we are committed to The Star Project, and will never abandon it or you. No matter how you see us… whether in robes, or in your dreams…, or in civvies", at that the three of them dropped their robes and stood before the crowd in Western clothes. "We are and always will be with you, all four of us. Please don't forget that". They picked up their robes and walked off stage. The audience didn't know how to react, so Mary rushed on stage, started to clap, and said, "Let the festivities begin!"

She was accustomed to the trio's occasionally bizarre behaviour, which was later in the day further evidenced by their reactions at the Tombola stall that was run by the local Scouts. The three of them had five or six goes each, but drew a booby prize every time. Nevertheless, far from being disappointed, it made them hoot with laughter. Anyone would have guessed that losing was the high point of their day.

The trio had great fun showing Siddhartha and Tara around the hospice. Tara joked that they had spent time in several hotels that were not up to its standard, and Siddhartha said that they had room to put a swimming pool around the back of the church, which everyone thought would be a good idea, when the funding became available. However, the two old grandparents were not as strong as they had been and soon tired.

"We're sorry, Carol, but my knees are throbbing now. I just can't get about like I used to".

"Yes, I'm getting tired too", said Tara. "We are going to have to make a move soon, before we collapse".

"Of course, thank you both for coming. It was really good of you. It just wouldn't have been the same if you hadn't been here".

"We wouldn't have missed it if we could help it", said Tara.

"If your leg is playing you up, grandfather, perhaps you would permit me to drive you home in your car; I can make my own way back here", offered Emrys because Tara had never learned to drive.

"We'll come with you", said Enaid for the both girls. "I am enjoying the atmosphere here, but I would appreciate a short break from the crowds and the noise".

"OK, thank you. I was a little concerned about driving. Whenever you are ready", said Siddhartha. The two elderly grandparents said their goodbyes, while Emrys went to fetch their car.

"The traffic is horrendous, isn't it, Emrys?" said Siddhartha en route.

"Yes. Friday evening… and there's an International on tomorrow".

"Oh, yes. I'd forgotten about that. Wales versus Ireland. I love the home International rugby games. Cardiff is buzzing when the pubs and streets are full of visitors. The Irish are one of the best… and the Scots… well, all of them really. The French, Italians… even the English!" he joked. The Welsh liked to pretend not to like the English in a jocular fashion when it was sure not to offend anyone, and Siddhartha had picked up the habit after so many decades in Wales. He would never have said it if it was likely to cause offence, since he was far too much of a gentleman for that, and didn't mean it anyway.

"Hello, Gāng Zhǎo", said Tara from the back seat. I was wondering were you had got to this afternoon" Siddhartha looked over his shoulder from the front seat and Emrys glanced in the rear-view mirror. The big cat was lying across the laps of the three ladies in the back seat. "It always amazes me how much stronger and braver I feel when Gāng Zhǎo is near me".

"We'll some have you home now… just a few more minutes…" said Emrys.

15. The End of an Era?

"Here we go!" said Alesha as she closed her eyes and gripped onto Gāng Zhǎo.

Bang!

There was an almighty bang and the dreadful sound of metal scraping over tarmac. By-standers looked away as an articulated lorry crashed into the side of Siddhartha's car and pushed it thirty metres up the road. There was nothing anyone could do to help except call the emergency services.

"No matter how many times I die", said Alesha, "it always makes me stiffen my muscles and hold my breath".

"Softie!" said Emrys.

"I know what's going on", smiled Alesha, "but I'm not a masochist. I don't mind being dead, but I don't want the dying bit to hurt"

"Softie!" he joked again.

"It's a bit like taking off or landing in a plane, isn't it? No matter how frequently you fly, there is always that brief moment of trepidation. It's funny that you should say that dying makes you stiffen your muscles and hold your breath, because that is exactly what the body does when you leave it. Rigor mortis sets in and breathing ceases!" said Tara.

"Yes, you're right. I'd never thought of that. Look at your lovely car, Siddhartha, it's a complete write-off!".

"We might as well move on", he replied "I don't like to see the old jalopy like that, and we are definitely brown bread… our bodies are only good for pushing up daisies now". Having said that, the five people and the tiger disappeared back to the hospice, and reappeared next to Carol, Sanjay, Mary and Jonathan, who were enjoying a glass of wine at a table. Carol was looking at her watch.

"Is it just me, or are they taking a long time to get back?"

"Perhaps they've stopped at Sanjay's Mum's for a cup of tea" said Jonathan.

"I hope so…"

"Phone them if you're worried", suggested Sanjay.

"I'll give them ten more minutes, but I'm not happy about something…"

"You feel it in your waters, do you?" joked Jonathan hoping to raise her spirits.

"Wait a second!" said Sanjay, "I'm pretty sure that I can see that tiger of theirs, Gāng Zhǎo… and five other shapes… figures, and a dog. Oh, my God! It's our children and my parents!"

"Does that mean that they are dead, or could they be only Astral Travelling?"

"I don't know how to tell, but something is going on". A few minutes later, the milling crowd parted and two police officers approached the table with Gail at their side. She gestured with her hand.

"Are you Mr and Mrs. Patel, and are you Mr and Mrs. Williams?" asked the female officer. They could only nod. "It is my sad duty to inform you that Mr and Mrs Patel senior, Emrys and Alesha Patel, and Enaid Williams have been involved in an accident".

"I don't like this bit either", said Alesha, looking on "it's heart-breaking".

Sanjay went ashen faced, but the other three wept openly. Gail and their friends that were standing nearby looked mortified.

They later found out that a lorry driver, who was behind schedule because of the extra traffic, had rushed through an amber light turning red, and hit the Patel's classic Mini Minor shooting brake broadside. The thirty-two ton truck travelling at thirty-five miles an hour had ploughed into the small car, and killed everyone inside it - probably instantly.

The truck driver had not been under the influence of drugs or alcohol, but he was found guilty of reckless driving and manslaughter. He was given the maximum custodial sentence under the law, but that was no comfort to the friends and family of the deceased. On the other hand, the deceased were very grateful to Mike, the driver, for helping them to leave Earth and move on, in spite of his having to go to gaol. He had said that he was looking forward to the intense experience of incarceration, when they had discussed his assistance with him years before.

∞

The funeral was a week later, and thousands of people, mostly teenagers, attended. They lined the streets from the Gateway Spiritualist Church where the ceremony took place to the Thornhill crematorium where they were to be cremated. Few people had seen a bigger procession or as many wreaths and flowers. They came in from all around the country where the trio had helped to establish other Star Projects during their brief sojourn on The Surface.

"I don't suppose we'll be riding back to Annwn on trusty steeds this time", said Emrys to his sister. The other three didn't understand, so Alesha explained.

"We can do, when we are all finished here, if we want to. You know that. Do you all fancy riding into town?"

"Whatever are we going to do without them?" Mary kept repeating throughout the day.

Sanjay was luckier, because he caught glimpses of the departed from time to time, and was able to comfort Carol with the news. He tried to help Mary and Jonathan too, but they were distraught, and not yet ready to be comforted. They locked themselves away in their house, and were not accepting phone calls or visitors for the foreseeable future. The death of their second daughter had hit them very hard. Luckily, the Star Project was able to continue under the leadership of the vice-chairperson, who was now Gail, and the Board of Directors.

The Patel's, on the other hand, had lost, in one single day, both children and Sanjay's parents, which also left the shops rudderless. Sanjay had to find the time to manage the shops, run his election campaign and help out at the SPC. Neither Sanjay nor Carol could afford themselves the luxury of wallowing in their grief.

"Don't ever forget that we have not left you!" was the message that the five dearly departed repeated the most often. They knew that Sanjay could see them, and thought that Carol would soon with Sanjay's assistance. Mary too, probably. Jonathan was an unknown as yet, although he did already believe in an Afterlife.

The number of attendees at the funeral was large, but the service was simple. Siddhartha and Tara had left instructions about what they wanted, but the trio had not. Nevertheless, their parents were sure that they would not have wanted anything elaborate either. So, since the five deceased were being cremated together, they also all received the same service that the grandparents had requested.

Carol chose the wording for their children's headstone, Sanjay chose for his parents, and the Williams's chose for Enaid. It was not difficult since the children had been prolific writers of Limericks and Haiku.

There were to be five separate headstones in the graveyard of the hospice, and a plaque inside it. Some board members proposed having a bronze statue of the trio placed in front of the hospice, but it was a question of finance. Sanjay and Carol were so touched by the suggestion and its support that they were considering selling one of the shops to pay for it out of their own pocket.

∞

In the short term, the SPC was blighted by a wave of grief and sorrow, but Sanjay and Carol worked hard to convince their colleagues that it was all part of 'The Plan' - the plan of the trio and many, many others too countless to mention. There was no doubt that the physical separation from their children was difficult, but deep down, they did understand that there was more 'going on' than was at first apparent.

It was especially difficult to deal with the hundreds of well-meaning people who commiserated with them that the trio had died 'too young'. Yes, their parents would have liked to enjoy their physical presence for much longer, but they could understand that Earth was not the best place for them to be, if they wanted to deliver the maximum benefit they could for the Souls of all the multiverses - the Star Children.

Leaving Annwn

16. Life Goes On

After the funeral, life on The Surface slowly returned to a form of 'normal' for those who had known 'The Star Children', as many came to call them. However, in reality nothing would ever be the same again. It is no exaggeration to say that the Earth would never be the same again, but this is true after the passing of every life. For, just as when a stone is cast into a pond, the pond seems to return to normal once the ripples have faded, the pond is in fact a little deeper. Yet the Star Children were no ordinary stones. They had had a massive effect on everyone who had met them, and on millions more who had not.

There were now thousands of Star Projects being established around the world, and they were all communicating with each other, sharing ideas, techniques and funds irrespective of national boundaries, languages, customs and governments, and Cardiff was the undisputed hub of this network. At first, Sanjay and Carol took on the rôles of communications officers, but it rapidly became too big for them to handle, so they had to hire a small team of professionals to man the phone lines, tend the blog, and answer emails concerning the activities of the project.

Other rôles previously done by volunteer Board Members also became paid jobs, and eventually the board decided that it was only fair to be paid in order to do properly what had become full time occupations. It was a big decision and not taken lightly. They were afraid that they would be seen to be profiteering from the project. However, that was not the case. In fact, the Board and the full time officials could now be expected to do a better job because they were being paid to do the work. The efficiency and level of service that the project was able to deliver soared.

Millions of people donated their time and money to help the organisation assist those less fortunate than themselves. Sanjay, Carol, Jonathan and Mary continued to play pivotal rôles in the movement until long after they had passed away from old age. The four parents made time to attend the Gateway Spiritualist Church every week, and a Development Circle there. They wanted to know more about psychic development, and they wanted to stay in touch with their loved ones.

At first, messages were conveyed to them from the entities that had been their recent family, but as they progressed, they too were able to see and hear them themselves. Sanjay was the most proficient at seeing Spirit, but Carol developed a talent for clairaudience that exceeded that of the others.

"It usually takes the recently departed a while to re-learn the techniques necessary to communicate with us on The Surface", explained Colin, the leader of the Circle. "The length of time varies a lot, but it seems to depend on the amount of skill that the departed had before and during their last life on Earth. Some find it hard to accept, but sometimes there is no desire to communicate with their previous Earthly friends, but it does happen. Let's face it, would you want to talk to everyone you've ever met, again? Some experiences just don't need to be repeated, do they?

"I'm not saying that that is going to happen to you. In fact, I know that it won't. I knew the children - I still think of them as children - anyway, I knew them very well, as you know. They had great love and respect for their parents. In fact, I never heard them say a bad word about anyone ever. They never complained… they were, are, quite remarkable".

Sanjay, Carol, Jonathan and Mary instinctively felt pride welling up within themselves, but were learning to try to repress it.

Sanjay was elected as the Member of the Senedd for his local constituency which included the area where he currently lived, and where the church and the hospice were located. He worked tirelessly to represent the interests of its inhabitants, businesses and institutions, which included the Star Project. In this way, he not only devoted time to the charity directly, but also indirectly through the Welsh government. He remained in the post until he volunteered to step down on his sixtieth birthday on the grounds that he wanted to devote more time to the Star Project International, and allow a younger person with 'new ideas' the opportunity to be heard in the Senedd.

Jonathan and Mary also continued to work at the Star Project, and go to the Development circle, but they had taken so long to recover from Enaid's death that Mary had to stand down from the position of chairperson - a decision that she later regretted. Further on, they were able to see and talk freely with Enaid, but never communicated with her twin. The consensus was that so much time had passed that she might have been reborn already, and so was busy with building a new life with other Souls somewhere in the vast infinity of the universes. However, they missed having youngsters around the house, and so became foster parents. The work was a pleasure to them, and helped them overcome their 'tragedy'.

Siddhartha and Tara were frequent visitors to the Development Circle. They took a keen interest in talking to the students there, and helping them see the World for what it really is. Tara especially liked to talk with the younger members. It was noteworthy that whenever they showed themselves they appeared less than half the age that they were when they passed over and always in traditional Indian costume from their region of birth. Tara wore beautiful saris of yellow, orange or gold, jewellery and a red dot, a bindi, on her forehead representing the Third Eye. Siddhartha always treated her with the utmost courtesy, and seemed like any young man who was besotted with his lady. His hair was finely coiffured, and he wore a handlebar moustache that was waxed and clipped. Furthermore, they usually walked arm in arm, something that the custom of their day on Earth had prevented them from doing in public.

They were radiant.

Kiddy was happy that Emrys, Alesha and Enaid were back. She had visited them often on the Surface, but had been busy comforting lonely and abused dogs, while they had been away. She had always enjoyed accompanying Emrys on his errands of mercy, and so filled in for him when he was otherwise engaged on The Surface. She and Gāng Zhǎo got on well, and enjoyed running and tumbling together in play. Gāng Zhǎo had developed a strange attachment to Cardiff because of Sanjay and Carol, and often visited the Gateway Development Circle. In fact, he was something of a celebrity with the students, and always created a stir. He was magnificent, and brought a sense of majesty, power and awe with him wherever he went.

Emrys, Alesha and Enaid remained close. They kept their most recent names, as well as their appearance as Buddhist initiates rather than going back to being Willy, Sarah and Becky, because most of the people who knew them as those entities had already passed over themselves.

They recovered from the shock of being reborn into Annwn quickly, and were soon back at their old jobs. Emrys cared for animals with his helper Kiddy; Alesha cared for 'lost' Souls, who didn't yet know that they were no longer on The Surface because of a sudden demise or just plain ignorance; and Enaid continued to work with the Star Project. In fact, they all devoted some time to the SPC, but it was Enaid's special interest, since it had been her idea in the beginning really. It was just a continuation of what she had been doing as Becky, but on a grander scale, although she could not have started the Star Project without a lot of help from people like Emrys, Alesha, Siddhartha, Tara, Sanjay, Carol, Jonathan, Mary and Michael, the lorry driver who had sent them home.

It proved unnecessary for Sanjay to have to sell one of his parent's shops to pay for a bronze statue, because the new chairperson of the board of SPC, Gail, suggested, and organised a collection for one. It seemed that the generous people of Cardiff were prepared to dig deep into their pockets to show their gratitude to the founders of the charity that had made their city world-famous again. Each Star Project sent a donation too.

The life size statue of a young Buddhist monk and two young Buddhist nuns with an elderly Indian couple in Namaste was placed in the front courtyard of the hospice with a fountain behind it, so that people passing by on the street would be treated to an image of the five people with a rainbow above and behind them when the sun shone. The effect was recreated at night with coloured lights. For those who were able to, Gāng Zhǎo and Kiddy could often be seen lying in the water under the fountain.

It was fittingly effective, and a source of great comfort to those who missed the 'dearly departed, but not forgotten'.

The End
(but not really ☺)

Leaving Annwn

Glossary

Barry: a large town to the west of Cardiff; now practically a suburb of it. It once exported a million tons of coal in a year – a world record that still stands – and was a very popular seaside resort.

Brecon: a market town near Cardiff.

Bristol: a large, historic port across the Bristol Channel from Cardiff.

Brown bread: Cockney rhyming slang meaning 'dead'.

Bryn: hill

Cardiff: capital of Wales, which is part of the UK

Cariad: love, lover, sweetheart, dear.

Coupy: squat

Custard slice : a popular sweet made of solid custard between layers of pastry topped with icing.

Gāng Zhǎo: a ghost Siberian tiger.

Kiddy: from *ci du* – Welsh for black dog (cwn=dogs).

Newport: an industrial city to the east of Cardiff

Senedd: The Welsh national government.

STAR Area of Cardiff: four local estates: Splott, Tremorfa, Adamsdown and Roath. It is completely unrelated to the Star Project in this novel.

Teg: fair

Twˆp: crazy, mad

Y Tywyth Teg: The Fair Family; The Fair People; the Fairies

Leaving Annwn

Bonus chapter of a new novel:

FATE TWISTER

The Strange Story of Wayne Gamm

by

Owen Jones

1 WAYNE GAMM

The screams coming from the secluded, old, stone farmhouse sounded inhuman, which was just as well, because the only red-blooded creatures that could hear them were four-legged, although they fully realised what was going on inside. Mrs. Gwynedd Gamm was having her first baby and her mother was helping her deliver it. The ewes in the field understood the pain Gwynedd was going through, even if her husband, Samuel Gamm and his drinking companions in the pub in the local village of Dremaelgwn did not.

"Mam! Get this baby out of me right now! Arghhh!"

"Try to relax, dear, and push… keep up the pressure…"

"Maybe I should have gone to the hospital to have him… we knew he was going to be a big, arghhh, baby!"

"Now, Gwynnie, we discussed that, didn't we, love? It was just not possible… far too dangerous. Just keep up the pressure, you're doing a great job, for a first-timer."

"Arghhh, oh, arghhh… uh, uh, uh, arghhh… Oh, Mum, he's huge! Arghhh, go in the kitchen, get the carving knife and cut me open… Go on, I don't care if you make a mess of it! Mam, I can't bear this any longer…"

"Yes, you can, Gwynnie, you have to, and you know that I can't help you like that as well… no-one can… That's why you have to have the baby here at home with no outsiders present.

"It was written, Gwynnie, you know that as well as I do. Hush now, Gwyn and concentrate, all women go through this and I promise you, that, one day, maybe in years to come, you will look back on this day with great pleasure."

"I'm, uh, arghhh, never going to have another one and that's for sure!"

"You say that now, my dear, but we'll see what happens, won't we, one day."

She had tried squatting in a warm bath, straddling a camping toilet seat, going on all fours and sitting on her haunches, but it was all the same, so she just lay on her back on her bed and tried to concentrate on moving her big baby boy out of her, millimetre by agonising millimetre. Gwynedd could feel his progress, but it was not fast enough for her.

"Give me some more of those tablets the doctor said I could take, Mam, please."

Her mother complied and then held a glass of cold water to her lips. Her face was dripping with perspiration.

Mother and daughter looked so alike that they could have been sisters, although on this day, it would have been a toss up, which one would have been guessed to be the older of them. There was only eighteen years gap between them and Gwynedd's mother, Rhiannon, kept herself looking very young for her age, as all women would if they had the choice, like she did.

The cottage and its lands had been in the family for longer than anyone could remember and they had a family Bible with everyone's name and the address of the farm in it that was 324 years old. Rhiannon, Rhiannon Phillips, owned it now and her daughter and new son-in-law lived with her, as was the local tradition. Mr. Phillips had long since passed away.

When asked what religion they belonged to, both Rhiannon and Gwynedd would say 'Chapel' automatically, and they didn't feel that they were being hypocritical. After all, it wasn't a bad religion, as religions went. It just didn't go far enough for them, because Rhiannon, her daughter and most people they knew, believed in a lot more.

Not only believed, but knew.

However, saying that they were 'Chapel' kept everybody happy and made the census forms easier to fill in. They even did go to Chapel whenever they could, even if it was only for the hymn-singing, but then so did everyone else as well. Even the Minister believed in more than he would admit to everyone, especially his superiors.

Rhiannon and her daughter were both gifted with 'second sight', as it was called, meaning that they could see into the future, and sometimes even into the past as well. It gave them a different perspective on time.

They both believed in Y Tylwyth Teg, or the Fairies in English, and regularly talked to the ones they believed were tending their garden and mountain they lived on, and they believed in fate, a pre-ordained future, which was why Gwynedd's baby was being born at home rather than in the hospital. They had both seen, in separate visions, that the baby, who would be called Wayne, would be 'large and special'.

They knew that Wayne would be special in a fashion that could go either way. They had seen that he could be dangerous – a handful in more ways than one.

They weren't sure of the details yet, but they had seen some awesome scenes, scenes that they did not want to become déjà vu. That was the last thing they wanted. They just could not be sure what would happen and that frightened them more than not having doctors or midwives around, to say nothing of the epidural pain-killers.

"That's the way, Gwynnie, come on, girl… I can see the top of little Wayne's head! Keep pushing!"

"Arghhh, arghhh, he… is not 'little' Wayne, his head feels the size of a rugby ball… arghhh, and that's not even the biggest part of him, is, uh, it? There's another two feet to go after that as well! I hope his shoulders aren't too broad yet. Oh, arghhh, never again, cut my tubes after this, Mam, phone up tomorrow, promise?"

"Come on, Wayne, help your mother to get you out, there's a good boy. Work with your son, Gwyn, come on both of you, work together, you're nearly there…"

"I've got him! Gwyn, I've got him! He's beautiful, he's perfect! Here, take your handsome son. Well done, both of you. My beautiful daughter and her handsome baby son."

Gwyn said a few words to Wayne and cwtched him close, but no-one except Wayne knew what she had said, but he answered with a cry. After a few minutes, Rhiannon took him back, cut the umbilical cord, cleaned him up, wrapped him in a blanket and handed him back to his mother. Then she went outside to get better reception and phoned Wayne's father.

"Sam, your beautiful son has arrived. Come on up and see him. He's perfect and Gwyn is well too."

He was more than a little drunk, but he did want to see his son.

"OK, Mam, I'll be there now." He clinked his glass with his two friends, finished his whisky and got in the van.

"We'll be off now too then, Sammy, congratulations, we'll call you tomorrow."

"All right, lads, thanks for keeping me company. See you tomorrow. Goodnight, be careful on those mountain roads now."

When he got home, which by pure chance was without having had an accident, he parked the car perilously close to the cottage and rushed inside.

"Oh, my dearest, Gwyn, you look a picture there, propped up in bed with our little shon, er… our Wayne. I'm sho proud of you both. Thanks,

Mam, for getting them both through thish. You can't guesh what I was thinking might be happening up here, you know, under the shircumshtances."

"Let me try to enlighten you then, Sammy, have you ever tried to pass anything this big on the toilet? I thought not, so, be a good boy and say no more… But, he is a lovely boy, isn't he? Mam, you were right, I don't regret any of that pain any more already."

"Can I get you anything, my darling, I am yoursh to command?"

"No, I don't want any more than I already have. Come and sit by us and put your arm around me, Sammy, but don't breathe over us. I don't want Wayne drunk on his first day out in the open."

Samuel moved his stool to the top of the bed, reached over and put his arm around his wife's shoulder. He held his breath, gazed into his son's face and thought that he had to be the happiest man on the whole of God's green Earth.

∞

Samuel was not from Wales, he had gone there from Cornwall one summer, four years before, in answer to an advertisement placed by the local sheep farmers for shearers. He had turned up on Rhiannon's farm and he and her daughter had fallen in love. Both Rhiannon and Gwyneth could see that it had been inevitable. There weren't many single people about, and certainly not within a twenty-minute ride, so when the handsome young man had stayed on the farm for a fortnight's shearing, it was, well, predictable, fate.

Rhiannon approved of him too. He was a knowledgeable sheep farmer, from sheep farming stock. He was tall and strong, and seemed besotted with Gwynedd. What more could a mother want for herself and her daughter? And Gwyn was too in love to care. She had led a lonely life on the mountain since leaving school and her mother understood that.

His only problem had been that he did not speak Welsh, but he was trying and the locals were giving him chance to learn, because he was a sheep farmer and because they all respected Rhiannon so much. There wasn't a family within fifty miles that had not had call to ask a favour of her at some time or another, and she never turned anyone away.

She was bringing Gwynedd up the same way, as her mother had done to her – ad infinitum, as far as anyone knew.

Samuel mixed and fitted in. He never argued about his workload, and seemed to relish being with the flock. The only thing was that he was used to drinking in his village public house in Cornwall after work, whereas where he was now was twenty minutes from Y Ddraig Goch – The Red Dragon, the nearest pub, and it did get him down sometimes.

Gwynedd had only ever been in a pub in Wales once and that was on her wedding day and she hadn't liked it much, even though she had been to school with most of the people in there. She had also had a drink with Samuel's mates in their village, but she had been happy to get out as soon as possible, although she did like his parents and phoned them more often than he did.

At twenty-two and twenty-five, Gwynedd and Samuel were a fairly typical, happy couple for the area with their first child and, being the offspring of farmers, they didn't think it unusual to live in their parent's house. In fact, Samuel appreciated Rhiannon being around and even enjoyed her company, and the feeling was mutual. The only thing that they did not quite 'see eye to eye on' was the supernatural, although Sam had said that his parents believed the same as Gwynedd's. However, Sam thought it 'old fashioned and stupid'.

He had said that to them both one night with a supercilious smile, that told both of the women that he was only giving the opinion of someone else, someone he admired. In other words, that he was talking through his hat. They both thought that he would grow out of it, when confronted with reality – the reality as they experienced it everyday.

He hadn't learned anything yet though that he could quantify that was not particular to hillside sheep farming in north Wales, but they still thought that he would come round eventually.

Rhiannon thought of herself as a white witch, that is a witch who would not harm anyone purely for self gain and Gwynedd liked to think that she was the same, but without the experience because of their ages. Rhiannon's mother had been a white witch and so had all the other matriarchs in their family, for ever, and every girl had been given the chance to learn.

Gwynedd had jumped at the opportunity to follow in their footsteps, as had her mother before her.

They didn't meet many people during the course of a typical week and most of them were known to them, but when they did meet strangers, or anyone for that matter, they would 'give them the once over' to see if they were on the level. Local people knew better than to try to cheat them, but the occasional travelling salesman might treat them like hicks, and they in their turn, considered them fair game to be taught a lesson.

Gwynedd remembered her father pleading with her once not to tell her mother that someone had sworn at him in a fit of road-rage when he was giving her a lift home from school one afternoon. She had been very young and not heeded the warning. She had related the incident to Rhiannon that night before going to bed and two days later the same man had skidded into a lamppost and was in a coma for months, although he did pull out of it.

Rhiannon had very intense powers of concentration and she looked after her own as everyone would like to be able to.

It had scared her husband into an early grave, because he was frightened to tell his wife anything, lest something happened and he would feel responsible.

He had been a good man and his conscience had not been able to bear that, no matter what anyone had done to him.

Samuel was the typical, proud, doting father with his new-born son, for the first few months. He and Gwynedd took Wayne into the hills with the sheep if the weather was fine and they took him to the market in the village on Saturdays when Sam would parade his baby around in his pushchair. However, gradually a feeling of rejection and even jealousy caused by the transformation of Gwynedd from a young lover into a mother caring for her first baby began to replace the pride of being a new father and Sam started to drink more, and with that he become more and more irritable.

Naturally, Sam didn't blame his son for this state of affairs, but he did start telling Gwynedd not to 'mollycoddle the boy' and several times he forced his attentions on her when she protested that she was too tired.

Gwyn was not happy with the way Sam was changing, but then she also knew that he was not happy with her either. Rhiannon tried to stay neutral and rarely said anything on the subject, but in reality she sided with her daughter and thought that Sam was being unreasonable.

Minor arguments soon became blazing rows with Wayne crying in his cot in the corner of the small living-room and his grandmother trying to pacify him. Sometimes, they would all be crying when they thought of what had become of their happy little family.

One evening, when Wayne was about six months old, Sam started an argument because his dinner was not to his liking, but he knew that that was only an excuse. He was shouting at Gwyn and standing over Wayne when he screamed:

"You care more about him than you ever did about me. You only want me around so's I can provide an income for our two witches and your precious baby. Neither of you give a damn about me any more, as long as I'm fit enough to go to work… Well, do you?" He was jabbing his finger at everyone including Wayne, who was becoming used to the tantrums and rarely cried any more.

"I can't eat that swill, I'm off to the pub!"

Neither of them remonstrated with him, because they knew that there was no point. He snatched the car keys off the mantelpiece and made for the door to the hall, but tripped over the tiny threshold, fell and hit his head hard on the wall in the hall opposite. Blood trickled from a lump forming rapidly on his forehead. With a loud curse, he picked himself up, opened the front door and slammed it behind him.

They listened in silence as the car started up and drove off at high speed. Then they smiled at each other.

"Serves him right!", said Gwyn and they both laughed. Wayne reacted to the change in atmosphere and began to chortle as well. They both looked at Wayne and said something appropriate for a baby.

"Sam will have a nasty bump tomorrow, he took quite a fall there and his headache will be more than just a hangover. He shouldn't have been so aggressive to little Wayne… You don't think that he had anything to do with Sam's fall, do you?"

"Sam is only jealous. He's just adapting to not being the only man in your life and not having your undivided attention. I'm sure he doesn't really blame anyone, it's quite normal. Isn't it?

"Are you thinking what I'm thinking about Sam's accident just now?"

"I think I am. We were both shown more than six months ago that it would be dangerous to upset Wayne, which was why I couldn't have him delivered in the hospital. If a strange doctor had slapped his bottom to start his breathing, who knows what might have happened? Still, it looks like we were being overcautious. Perhaps, his powers are only just starting to wake up."

"Have you ever warned Sam about Wayne?"

"No, it wasn't necessary at first and then, when the rows started, nothing happened, and I just sort of forgot."

"He will need to be told, Gwyn."

"Yes, I know, Mam, I'll do it as soon as we're talking again, but that fall could just have been an accident… Perhaps, he wouldn't hurt his own father."

"We don't know, do we, Gwyn? We just don't know that yet, my dear."

It was two days later that she had the chance to talk to her husband. Gwyn had arranged for her mother to give them thirty minutes of privacy, but to then come in so that she could ask her to confirm what she had said, as if unrehearsed.

"…and that's the long and the short of it, Sammy. You know that Mam and I have the second sight, you believe that already. Well, we were both shown that Wayne would be able to cause things to happen… perhaps things from someone's own future, to compress their fate, or give it a twist, so to speak. We've been waiting for evidence that it is true.

"Your fall the other evening after losing your temper in front of Wayne and pointing at him like that, may have been the first instance of him performing or it could have been a pure accident, we don't know.

"I'm only saying this for your own safety, so you can't say that I didn't warn you. I think that you ought to take care, cariad. I love you and don't want anything to happen to you."

"Well, thanks for the warning, but I don't believe that that is possible, my dear. I have respect for your powers and your mother's, but you must both have got it wrong this time. You make our little Wayne sound like one of the X Men, but he's not. He's just a lovely little boy, who has turned our lives upside down and I hate myself for feeling bitter about it sometimes, but that's how it is. I do feel like that sometimes, and I know that it's wrong, but… I suppose I'm only a man, not an X Man, and I miss not getting all my beautiful wife's attention and the only one I can blame is little Wayne. I know it's not his fault, and I hate myself for thinking it.

"We made Wayne, you and me, and I know that you have to take care of him, I know all that, but knowing it doesn't make the loneliness any easier to bear."

"I know, my dear, but I'm sure that what I have told you is correct. Mam feels the same as well."

Rhiannon entered right on cue.

"Mam, I was just talking to Sam about Wayne being special. Could you tell him what you think? Perhaps, that will persuade him."

Rhiannon told the same story but in her own words, and Sam came a little closer to believing them.

"But he's not going to hurt his own family, is he? It just doesn't make sense that he should bite the hands that feed him."

"Fate shows no favouritism, Sam. Whoever does wrong gets repaid in like kind, as do those who do good, whoever they are, family of not.

Universal laws operate the same for everyone, and anyway, not all parents are good to their children. Some kids suffer all sorts of abuse from their family.

"If Wayne can somehow have an influence over how quickly that fate catches up with them, well, it's not as if people are not getting something that they don't deserve, it's just that they are getting it a bit earlier. The way I see it, he cannot change fate, no-one can, but maybe he can twist it so that the order in which events take place changes."

"We're not sure of all the details yet, darling, it is still early days, but it is our best guess so far."

"Do you think that he knows that he can do it?"

"I shouldn't think so, he's only a six-month old baby, but he is growing up fast and his powers may develop quickly too. We just don't know, this is a new situation for all of us."

"Yes, it sure is! Especially if what you say is right. I'll have to have a think about what you've said and in the meantime be very careful how I behave around Wayne."

"Good, just keep your eyes open, because we believe that Wayne's powers are starting to become active. It might be a good idea to keep him out of stressful situations, until we better understand what's going on."

The following Saturday, while walking in town, an incident occurred which went a long way towards convincing Sam that his wife and mother-in-law were right. Sam was pushing the pram across the road on a Zebra Crossing. He had reached the policia beacons in the middle of the road, checked the traffic and was half way across the second lane when a speeding car appeared out of nowhere.

He froze for a second or two not knowing whether to go on or to go back and all the while the solitary car was bearing down on them at speed. At the very moment that he decided to go back to the safety of the beacons and give the car enough room to pass by, it veered sharply to the left and crashed into a concrete lamp post full on. The car stopped dead and the lamp post cut a deep V-shape in the bonnet and engine, but the driver was only badly shaken, not physically hurt.

He later admitted in an interview with the local newspaper that he had been speeding and driving while intoxicated, but he claimed to have lost control of his vehicle seconds before it crashed into the lamp post. He also remarked that if he had not been wearing his seat belt, he would have been killed. He even gave a public apology to the Gamm family and said that he had never been so scared in his whole life as when he found himself bearing down on the father and baby and lost control of the steering.

Sam had noticed that his son had looked rather 'worried' as the car had approached them with its horn blaring, but he assumed that he had been picking that up from him, since Sam admitted to being very frightened for them both. When Sam had finished relating his story, Gwyn and Rhiannon looked at each other knowingly and Sam knew that they thought that Wayne had caused the car to crash.

He had to admit that it could look that way, especially in the light of what they already believed. He looked at his son who was sitting up in his cot playing with some plastic animals that were hanging from a cord strung across it. There was nothing in his demeanour to suggest anything other than that he was trying to amuse himself playing with his toys on his own.

There would follow many minor instances which proved nothing taken as solitary occurrences, but which together gave a strong indication that Rhiannon and Gwynedd were right about Wayne and his nascent powers.

The biggest problem they had though, apart from the arguing, which had decreased, was how to integrate Wayne into society. He was still only six months old and would not have to go to school for about five years, but the way things were going, he wouldn't know any other children or how to behave correctly when he did meet any.

One thing they did know though was that they couldn't just throw him into a classroom of strangers and expect everything to go all right. He had to learn the concepts of give and take and sharing, and how to control his temper, if he had a bad one.

About the Author

Owen Jones, Amazon Best-Selling author from Barry, Wales, has lived in several countries and travelled in many more. While studying Russian in the USSR in the Seventies', he hobnobbed with spies on a regular basis. After university, in Suriname, he got caught up in the 1982 coup, when he was accused of being a mercenary.

Later, while a company director, he joined the crew of four as the galley slave to sail from Barry to Gibraltar on a home-made concrete yacht during Desert Storm. En voyage, the yacht was almost rammed by a Russian oil tanker, and an American aircraft carrier - The Atlantic Challenger.

Since 2004, he has lived mainly in the UK, Spain and Thailand. He now leads a somewhat quieter life in his wife's remote, northern farming village writing, editing and increasing the number of translations, and narrations of his novels.

As he says: "Born in the Land of Song, living in the Land of Smiles".

A Proud Celt

"I am a Celt, and we are romantic", he said when asked about his writing style, "and I firmly believe in reincarnation, Karma and Fate, so, sayings like 'Do unto another...', and 'What goes round comes around' are central to my life and reflected in my work. I write about what I see, or think I see, or dream... and, in the end it is all the same really". He speaks seven languages and is learning Thai, since he lives in Thailand with his Thai wife of nineteen years.

Early Career

In 2004, he started his first novel, *Daddy's Hobby* (from the seven-part series *'Behind The Smile: The Story of Lek, a Bar Girl in Pattaya'*), but he didn't finish it until 2012. However, his largest collection is '*The Psychic Megan Series*', twenty-three novelettes on the psychic development of a teenage girl, the subtitle of which, '*A Spirit Guide, A Ghost Tiger and One Scary Mother!*' sums them up nicely. However, since 2012, he has written fifty-odd novels and novelettes, including the military drama *Dead Centre*; the spy novel *Andropov's Cuckoo*; a fantasy *Fate Twister*; a philosophical vampire comedy *The Disallowed*; a whodunnit *Tiger Lily of Bangkok*; and Spiritualist drama, *A Night in Annwn* (Annwn being the ancient Welsh word for Heaven). Not only that, but many have been translated into foreign languages and narrated into audio books. In fact, he has over 1,200 books and novels credited to him at the British Library.

You can find his many other novels on:

https://meganpunlishingservices.com

Owen Jones

Books by the same author

Behind The Smile:
The Story of Lek, a Bar Girl in Pattaya
Daddy's Hobby
An Exciting Future
Maya – Illusion
The Lady in the Tree
Stepping Stones
The Dream
The Beginning

-

The Disallowed
Chupacabras on Backpacker Blood-Milkshake
http://thedisallowed.com

-

Tiger Lily of Bangkok
When the Seeds of Revenge Blossom!
Tiger Lily of Bangkok in London
The Tiger Re-awakens!

-

Alien House
A Story of Love, Despair, and Alien Intervention!

-

Andropov's Cuckoo
A story of Love, Intrigue, and The KGB!

Leaving Annwn

-

A Night in Annwn
The Strange Story of Old Willy Jones' Near-Death Experience

Life in Annwn
The Story of Willy Jones' Life in Heavenly

-

Fate Twister
The Story of Wayne Gamm
http://fatetwister-waynegamm.com

-

Dead Centre
Not Every Suicide-Bomber Is Religious!

Dead Centre 2
Even The Wrong Can Be Right Sometimes!

-

Alien House
A Story of Love, Hope and Alien Intervention

-

Daisy's Chain
A Story of Love, Intrigue and The Underworld on The Costa del Sol

-

The Bull at the Gate
The Day the Sky Fell

-

The Psychic Megan Series
A Spirit Guide, A Ghost Tiger, and One Scary Mother!

The Misconception
Megan's Thirteenth
Megan's School Trip
Megan's School Exams
Megan's Followers
Megan and the Lost Cat

Megan and the Mayoress
Megan Faces Derision
Megan's Grandparents' Visit
Megan's Father Falls Ill
Megan Goes on Holiday
Megan and the Burglar
Megan and the Cyclist
Megan and the Old Lady
Megan's Garden
Megan Goes to the Zoo
Megan Goes Hiking
Megan and the W. I. Cookery Competition
Megan Goes Riding
Megan and the Radio One Beach Party
Megan Goes Yachting
Megan At Carnival
Megan's Christmas
Megan Catches Covid-19

Look here for the latest list of books in
The Psychic Megan Series
A Spirit Guide, A Ghost Tiger, and One Scary Mother!
http://tinyurl.com/meganseries

-

Non-Fiction:

How to Give Your Dog a Real Dog's Life
and make him love you for it!

-

The Eternal Plan
– Revealed
(written by Colin Jones, compiled by Owen Jones)

-

Authorship
Publishing Your Book On You Own
http://owencerijones.com

For more information about my books and free audiobook copies, please visit my blog at:
https://meganpunlishingservices.com

Review Request

Please write a review of this book, and the series, if you have read the trilogy, because your impression matters a lot to me and other readers. Don't underestimate the power of voicing your opinion.

Best wishes,

Owen Jones

www.ingramcontent.com/pod-product-compliance
Lightning Source LLC
Chambersburg PA
CBHW070736020526
44118CB00035B/1387